43

HOUSES

THE JACKAL

Copyright © 2024 by
The Jackal

Printed in the United States of America

Published by Book Marketeers.com

DEDICATION

For those who love the hunt just as I do.

ACKNOWLEDGMENT

To all sociopaths, narcissists, psychopaths and serial killers. We are always family.

Table Of Contents

Introduction

One of the questions I get so many times is, "Is it scary being a Serial Killer?" "Aren't you afraid to get caught?" The answer to both is no. I've been killing since I was seven years old. I'm almost 60. I haven't gotten caught yet. Arrested under suspicion but never convicted. I'm sure I'm under their radar, but that just makes the game more fun.

The high is always there; at least for me, it is not like the first time. The first kill is always your best. It's raw and exciting. You chase after it for the rest of your life. You come close to that feeling, but you never quite experience that first feeling.

It's like having sex for the first time. Driving a car for the first time. Going to Disney for the first time. Taking off in a plane for the first time. It's exciting. Scary. Exhilarating. All at once. Then you chase that feeling again and again.

Some Serial Killers get caught up in that feeling, and when they can't find it, they get frustrated and make mistakes. You must control your emotions. Lavish in the hunt and then the kill. Still don't get what I'm explaining? Ok, go back to the example of the plane.

First time on a plane you go to the airport. You see planes come and go as you drive up into the parking lot. You start to have a bit of anxiety, knowing that you will be on a plane in less than three hours. You park and walk up to the door, full of anticipation. You go through baggage and then through security. You sit in your area and go to the bathroom three times because you're nervous. They make several announcements about when your plane will be boarded. They finally announce its time to board. You wait for your section to be called. You're already standing and fidgeting because you can't relax.

You give them your ticket to scan and then you walk down the corridor to the door of the plane. Once you cross that door, you can't turn back. You find your seat and get comfortable. Finally, after several minutes, they shut the door, and the plane eventually starts to line up at the runway. The plane finally takes off like a shot, and within moments, you're in the air. You will feel accomplished and exhilarated over the experience. The next time you fly, you get some of that feeling back, but not 100%. You get 85%. Then, the next time, you get 75% and so on.

It's the same with killing. You pick a target and plan. You watch your target for days, sometimes longer. When the time is right, you stalk your target and slowly coral them where you need them to be. You let them see you, so they get nervous and make mistakes making them easier to coral. You do this alone or with a willing partner.

Eventually, you get them to the spot you need them to be and corner off every available exit. You talk to them very calmly, watching them panic. This is part of the game. They will be excited, angry, and crying and finally, they will try to negotiate with you for their release. This is when you are the calmest.

You either release them and catch them again and play with them like a cat does with a mouse until you're ready to commit and kill them, or you tie them up and torture and kill them. Each killer is different in their method as they are different in their choice of weapon.

Once you cross that line, you can't go back. Once you kill, it's done. It's not like the movies. There is no music in the background playing. It's just you and them. Once they're dead, you still have the murder weapon to deal with. The body to remove and the area to clean. Moving a dead body is not easy.

Unless, of course, you have a clean-up crew to call. Or a partner to help you. That is why connecting with other Serial Killers is important. A support system. Kind of like going to church. You go to church to connect with like-minded people who worship God. But you go to a church that believes in the same beliefs as you have. Catholic. Jewish. Mormon.

Serial Killers also connect with like-minded and meet. They also sometimes live very close to each other. I live in community 43. It's relaxing knowing that my neighbors are always committed to me as I am committed to them. What's even better is when the prey comes to you.

Chapter 1

Isaac poked the fire with a stick. The smell of burning wood relaxed him. He secretly wished he had brought marshmallows, but with the mood everyone was in tonight, he was glad he didn't. He looked up at the stars. He could see his breath. It was a brisk evening. He looked back at the fire and then the circle of friends who had gathered.

"Ok, we're all here to say goodbye to Logan." Darren begins. Everyone nods.

"Wait," Madeline looks around. "Shouldn't we wait for the others to come?"

Several shrugs. "No one else is coming," Russell remarks. "It's always been just us."

Madeline nods in agreement and pushes sand toward the rocks that circle the fire pit.

Hayden passes out the tin mugs he brought and puts coke in each one. He then grabs a bottle of rum from his back pocket and raises it for all to see. He shakes it and smiles. No one smiles back. Sensing the seriousness of why they were all there, he stops and nods. He takes off the wrap and pours a little in each cup.

"I think we should say something," Lilly began, looking around the group at each member. "I mean something positive about Logan."

Everyone nods. No one says anything, so Lilly begins. She raises her cup. "To Logan. You helped me get through Miller's Math class. You always had a great joke to tell, and you always wore that green hoody your grandfather gave you." She smiles.

Everyone smiles and raises their mugs. They all take a sip. Madeline looks around, then begins. "To Logan. Who saved me from drowning in Elk Creek two years ago when I slipped down the hill. I hit my head. You saved my life," she smiles. She looks over at Russell who looks at her. "And to you,

Russell for knowing first aid." He grins. They all drink.

Russell raises his mug. "To Logan, who wanted out of this God-forsaken dump of a town. Who did everything right even when everything was stacked against him. You did things your way. Just like you should." Everyone nods.

Madeline sniffles. "No tears," Isaac points at her. "He knew what he was doing. I mean, chemo is expensive. His parents couldn't afford it. I understand why he did it."

"Did you know he was going to kill himself, Isaac?" Lilly asks concerned.

Isaac thinks and shakes his head no. "I really didn't. Hayden and I were thinking of starting a GoFundMe account for him."

Hayden shakes his head in agreement. "That's right. We were also going to ask the coach and the principal if we could do some school rallies to raise money for the chemo treatments."

Lilly sighs. "Corporations suck," she mumbles. Everyone nods.

Hayden raises his glass. "To Logan. Our friend. Forever. Till we meet again. Fly high buddy." They all hit their mugs together and down the rest of their drinks.

"This stuff sucks," Darren remarks, and everyone laughs.

They all sit down by the fire and laugh and talk. "We all graduate this year," Lilly remarks. "What are we all going to do? I mean, some of us won't see each other ever again."

"No, that's not true," Madeline replies.

"Yes, it is," Ella remarks. "I mean, we'll have the summer, but some of you will go off to college. Mostly out of state."

"That's true," Russell remarks as they all laugh. "Way out of state. Across the country."

"Some of us are stuck here to get jobs," Ella looks around the woods.

"This place isn't that bad," Hayden remarks. His remark is returned with stares and glares. "What? We have a McDonalds, a movie theater, a bowling alley. What else is there." Everyone bursts out laughing.

"A lot, dude. A lot more out there," Isaac says. "The ocean, the country. Big cities. Bigger and better jobs. That's just a few things."

Hayden shrugs. "I know. But not everyone is athletic or beautiful or talented," he replies as he looks at each of them when he says it.

"So, I'm beautiful?" Russell jokes.

Everyone laughs. "No, you are athletic dude," Hayden rolls his eyes.

"Dude, you can leave, you know?" Russell points at him.

"No, I can't. Most of us can't. Our parents…." Hayden begins.

"Fuck your parents, man," Russell yells. Everyone looks shocked. Lilly looks scared.

"You have to stand up to them. You have to live your life and not their missed dreams. You take those opportunities and run with them."

"Says the guy who has the college scholarship wrapped up," Ella reminds him.

Russell grits his teeth. "Hey, I earned that. I worked hard. I got up every morning since grade school and worked out before school. Then, after school, I did football. Then came home and did homework, and then my Dad ran drills with me."

"Key word there, sport," Hayden points at him. "Your Dad ran drills. He pushed you. He wanted this just as much as you did."

"Is that what you really want to be when you leave here?" Lilly asks him. Russell looks at the group and at her. He looks down. "Deep down inside, do you want to be a football player?"

Russell shakes his head no. Isaac sits up straighter. "What do you really want to be?" Isaac asks, interested.

Russell shrugs, obviously embarrassed to tell the group. "Dude, we're not going to laugh," Darren tells him.

Russell sighs. "I want to be a nurse. But in the city." Everyone ponders what he says. Lilly smiles.

Lilly claps her hands. "That is so cool. You would make a great nurse." Russell smiles.

"Then become a nurse," Isaac tells him. "I mean, you have a college scholarship for playing football. Just take classes for nursing." Everyone nods.

Russell laughs. "They sent me the college curriculum and I filled out the first year of the basics on what they expect you to take. The second year, you can start taking a class here and there on what you'd like, and I put in Anatomy and Biology and my Dad saw it and erased it and put in weight training and nutrition."

Hayden shakes his head. "Parents are such control freaks."

"When are they going to let us grow up and make our own decisions?" Isaac asks.

"Did you tell your Dad you wanted to be a Nurse?" Lilly asks him.

Russell shakes his head no. "I mean, last month, my little brother and I got into a fight. Nothing big. Just goofing around, and we got out of control. He ran to my Mom and said you know Russell wants to be a nurse and not a football player. She said, what? You know how much football players make and how much nurses make? I said well, nurses save lives, don't get hurt on the field and make a difference. I could go anywhere with a degree. She looked at me and said boy, your daddy and I put years of our lives into your career. Into your future. You're not going to let us down." Russell stares at the ground and kicks dirt into the fire.

Lilly sighs. "mine expect perfect grades."

"I'm supposed to go into the family business of painting," Darren replies.

"Mine, ignore me," Madeline says sadly. Lilly hugs her. Darren pats her back.

"Factory worker for life here," Hayden raises his hand.

"How do I tell my parents I want to be a priest?" Darren asks. Isaac's eyes open wide.

"Are you kidding, dude?" Hayden asks. Darren shakes his head no.

"Wow, that's tight man," Russell remarks.

Lilly smiles. "I think it's wonderful." Ella hugs Darren.

Isaac nods, and Madeline smiles. "Father Darren. It has a nice ring to it." she says. Everyone laughs. They all start to dance around the fire.

As they do, Isaac missteps and falls to the side. "Are you ok dude?" Hayden goes to him to help him up.

As Isaac gets up, he sees a work van on the side of the road being pulled over by the police. The policeman gets out of his vehicle and walks over to the Van. The man in the Van is rearranging his front seat. Both boys watch.

"Oh, someone just got pulled over," Isaac shakes head.

"Poor sap," Hayden says. "I bet he was speeding."

"Who cares?" Isaac whispers. "No one is on this road this late."

The officer motions the man out and does a sobriety test on him. The man stumbles. "Oh shit," Isaac laughs.

"He's screwed," Hayden laughs. "Now they're going to take him away, and he'll lose his job."

"Jobs are hard to come by in this town," Isaac nods in agreement. The officer places the man on the side of his car and cuffs him after searching him.

Hayden drinks a little more and starts getting tipsy. He throws out the rest of the drink into the grass and blinks several times. Isaac laughs at him and looks back at the Van. "Listen to what he's saying," Isaac says.

"Yeah, I'm going to take him. The tow truck won't be here for two hours. They're taking care of an accident on I-95. The Van will be ok here. No one is here." Cop says into his radio mic on his shoulder. He looks around.

Both boys squat down. Isaac looks over at the others. The fire has already died down, and they are covering it with dirt. Isaac looks back at the cop as he goes back into the vehicle. Hayden squints his eyes to read the side of the guy's Van.

"Locksmith. He's a Locksmith." Hayden repeats.

Isaac stands and smiles. "I have an idea."

Hayden sees his look and looks back at the Van and at Isaac. "No," Hayden shakes his head. "No. We'll get caught. We'll go to jail. Our parents will be pissed."

"What are they going to do? Ground us and make us stay here forever?" Isaac asks. "Besides, the cop says the tow truck won't be here for 1-2 hours. We're right here. We walk right there. Take the key and leave. No one will know."

"Take a van?" Hayden points to the Van. Hayden looks as the cop car was now gone. "What are we going to do with a van full of keys?"

"Not the van and not all the keys," Isaac starts down the hill. He stops and grabs Hayden's shirt and pulls him along. "Just one key. The master key."

"Master key?" Hayden asks.

"Yeah, the master key fits every key lock in the world. We get that, and we're set." Isaac tells him.

"Set to do what exactly Isaac?" Hayden asks. But he already knew the answer. Isaac wanted to steal stuff from people's houses.

"Look, we both need to get the hell out of this town," Isaac begins. "We take that key, and we hit some rich people's houses and stop."

Hayden shakes his head no. "Absolutely not," Hayden tells him.

"Why?" Isaac asks.

"First, it's illegal. Second, it's wrong. Third, everyone in this town knows everyone. We'll eventually get caught." Hayden begins. "And I could stand here all day giving you forty more reasons."

Isaac pulls Hayden down the slope to the van door. Hayden is still giving him reasons why they shouldn't. "People have video cameras. People have guns."

"What are they doing?" Ella asks, looking over the embankment.

"What are you guys doing?" Madeline yells down to them.

"Shut up," Hayden yells back. "Someone will hear you."

"Who?" Russell holds his hands up.

"They're going to break into that Van. Oh my God," Lilly looks around.

"Just keep watch," Isaac yells back up to them. The others look around. Russell shakes his head.

Isaac tries the front door and it opens immediately. "Dude, they didn't lock it," he tells Hayden.

"He probably didn't think he was going to get arrested. Shit, dude there are a lot of keys in here," Hayden says, looking around.

"Go on the other side," Isaac pushes him and goes inside the Van. Hayden goes to the other side, and Isaac unlocks the door. Isaac sits behind the driver's seat and surveys the front area while

Hayden sits carefully in the front with the side door open, surveying the back.

Russell looks around and back down at the Van. "White people are so crazy," he says.

"They're going to get caught," Lilly tells everyone.

"From who?" Darren raises his arms. "No one is here," he adds, looking in every direction.

"You're ok with this, Father Darren?" Madeline asks. Russell laughs and looks at Darren.

"I'm not a priest yet." he replies. They all laugh.

"Here it is," Isaac says, opening a container with a key inside it. As he takes the key out, a small red light is on in the front of the dash above the radio. Neither of the boys sees it. The light connects to a camera, and from behind the camera, a recording of them is being made that neither of them is aware of.

"Car!" Russell yells and points. The others start pointing in the same direction. Hayden looks and points and jumps out slamming the door shut.

Isaac looks and gets out, but something catches his eye. A black notebook tucked in the side by the front seat on the panel. He grabs it and the key, shuts the door and runs to the back of the Van and into the bushes.

Hayden beats him up the hill. The others squat and watch to see if the driver notices them, but he does not. It's the tow truck. It turns and backs up to the Van. The driver opens his car door, writes information down and then gets out and begins hooking up the Van, oblivious to the fact that the Van had been ransacked.

Isaac comes up from the side of the hill, and all of them take off for home. "You're crazy," Lilly tells them as they run down the hill toward the town.

"Crazy as a fox," Isaac laughs.

"What did you take out of the Van?" Madeline asks.

"A key to our future," Isaac holds up the key with one hand and then holds up the black notebook. "And a way out of this town."

They get to the park, stop at a picnic table, and sit at it. "What did you mean a way out of this town?" Ella asks.

"This key is the Master key. The Van was a locksmith van. So, this key is special. Every Locksmith gets one of these. This key can open any door in America." Isaac proudly says.

"So what?" Darren replies.

"They're gonna rob people's houses," Russell tells Darren. Darren looks at them, and Isaac nods yes while Hayden shakes his head no.

"I won't do this, Isaac," Hayden tells him. Isaac is busy looking through the book. "Do you hear me, Isaac?"

"Isaac, think about this," Lilly tells him. "If you get caught, your life is over."

Russell nods. "Yeah, man. These are hard-working people. You want to steal from them?"

Isaac holds his finger up. He begins to count. "He's not listening," Darren says.

"Yes, I am. I'm just counting. Give me a sec." Isaac tells them. They all watch him.

"It's almost curfew, guys," Madeline tells them. "Not like my family cares," she mumbles.

"Yes, they do," Darren tells her. She rolls her eyes.

"There are 43 houses listed here. That's it." Isaac looks perplexed.

"Maybe he just started his business," Ella suggests. Isaac nods.

"Most of them are out of town. On the outskirts of the city, but also in the middle of nowhere." Isaac tells him.

"We're not doing this," Hayden tells him.

"What if we just drive by one? If it's a rich house, we hit that. Just the rich one." Isaac suggests.

Hayden shakes his head no. The others look at each other. Isaac looks at Russell. Russell eyeballs him. "Hell no. I have a scholarship. I mess up, and I lose that." Russell reminds him.

Isaac looks at each of them. Lilly shakes her head no. Madeline shrugs her shoulders, and Isaac smiles. Darren says no, and so does Ella. Finally, he looks at Hayden.

"Dude, we've done stuff since grade school," Isaac reminds him.

"Yeah, but nothing like this," Hayden says. "Look, I'll go with you, but I'm telling you I don't feel right about this."

"One house," Isaac says, holding up one finger. "And only if it's clear. Like no one home. Only if it's a rich house." Hayden nods as Lilly rolls her eyes.

They all say goodbye and leave. Isaac walks home and goes to bed, holding the black book. He counts the entries. 43 addresses. 43 possibilities. He drifted off to sleep.

Chapter 2

Taking a Chance

Isaac awoke to the sound of the neighbor's dog barking. He stretched then checked his clock. 1030 a.m. He had slept in. He put on some pants and got out of bed. As he did, the black notebook fell onto the ground. He picked it up and smiled. He sat it on the table by his keys and went downstairs.

"Mom? Dad?" Isaac yelled. No answer came back. He opened the fridge and glanced around. Isaac pulled out the orange juice and drank several gulps from the container. He shut the fridge door and looked to see Calistoga, his cat watching him. "Don't tell mom," Isaac said out loud, laughing.

Isaac walked over to the phone and saw a piece of paper by the answering machine. "Isaac, your Dad and I went to the city for the day. See you tonight at dinner. Mow the lawn. Love Mom and Dad." Isaac sighed and rolled his eyes.

He went outside to check the weather. It was already starting to warm up. He did not want to mow the lawn. He wanted to go to the Drive-In and grab a burger and some fries. He wanted to hang with friends. He wanted to drive to the city and walk around. But no, he had to mow the lawn. He looked at his little brother.

"Why don't you mow the lawn." Isaac asked him.

"I'm 11," Martin replied. He continued reading his comics.

"How much is that new videogame you want?" Isaac asked him. Martin sat up immediately.

"A lot. Like $35," Martin said hopefully. Isaac nodded.

"You mow the lawn, like right now, rake it and bag everything, and I'll give you $40, but you can't tell Mom and Dad you did it. I did it." Isaac takes out his wallet from his jeans and shows Martin two $20's.

"Deal," Martin yells and throws the comic down. Isaac smiles and sets the money inside the comic. Martin watches him do it. Isaac points to the garage, and as Martin takes off to do his brother's job, Isaac goes upstairs to finish getting dressed. He grabs the notebook and his cell phone and heads to his car.

Inside his car, he texts Hayden that he's on the way and takes off. Within ten minutes, he was in front of Hayden's house. Hayden was already outside, sitting on the porch steps, waiting for him.

"I'm starving," Hayden tells him.

"Good cause I haven't eaten yet," Isaac tells him.

"I got money," Hayden offers. "I got lunch."

"Drive-In ok?" Isaac asks. Hayden points onward.

"Heard from the girls this morning yet?' Hayden asks.

Isaac shakes his head no. "I just woke up. My parents left a note. They're in the city all day, but they wanted me to mow the lawn. I got Martin to do it."

"How old is he now?" Hayden asks.

"He's 11 years old," Isaac tells him.

Hayden shrugs. "I did the lawn at ten. He'll be fine. How much you pay him?" Hayden grins.

Isaac looks at him. "What makes you think I paid him?"

"How much?" Hayden asks again. Isaac laughs.

"$40" Isaac tells him.

Hayden sits up. "$40! Hell, I would have done it for you dude." Hayden laughs.

"We've got better things to do," Isaac holds up the black notebook. Hayden sighs. Isaac pulls into the Drive-In and pulls into an open slot.

The boys quickly survey the cars to see if they know anyone. "There's Katie," Hayden waves at her. She waves back.

"She's with Tim, isn't she?" Isaac asks. Hayden nods.

"He's going into the Marines. She's going to community college to become a baker." Hayden tells him.

"Nice," Isaac says. "Oh my God, there's Tabitha Johnson." Isaac looks away.

"Where?" Hayden asks and then sees her. "Shit, look away." Tabitha honks her horn four times, and the boys finally wave to get her to stop. "What a nut." They both laugh.

"What are you getting?" Isaac asks.

"Get me a double cheeseburger, large onion ring and a large Dr. Pepper," Hayden tells him. Isaac orders two of the same.

As they wait for their order, they look through the black notebook. "Look, we'll go to this house today and just drive by. See what it looks like and what the area looks like." Isaac tells Hayden.

Hayden thinks and tells him, "Ok, but listen, if we see anyone, and I mean even a dog, we're gone." Isaac nods, and they knuckle bump.

They eat their food, and they're on their way. "I can't believe the girls haven't called yet." Isaac tells Hayden.

"Probably still sleeping," Hayden replies.

They drive for about 40 minutes when Isaac tells Hayden to check the address on the first house. "I think this is the turnoff up here."

"What if we get down there, and the house is the only one on the block, and someone comes out?" Hayden asks.

"We'll just tell him or her we're lost." Isaac explains.

"What if…." Hayden starts, but Isaac cuts him off.

"We'll tell them that we're just driving and looking at the countryside. Looking for houses to buy or something. Jeez, dude, stop being paranoid." Isaac snaps.

"Calm down. Yeah, here's the turn, and there's the house. There's another house up ahead about a couple of miles. Let's just go toward that one and glance over at this one." Hayden suggests.

"Ok, here we go," Isaac turns. "My heart's pumping."

"So is mine," Hayden says. The boys turn down the road. About ten seconds into the road, they pass a house on the left, which is listed in the notebook. The house is blue with white trim. A white picket fence runs around the front of the house. No fence in the back. There is no car in front but a garage in the back that is big enough to hold several cars and possibly a boat. In the back is a dog house, but no dog. The boys continue on for about five minutes, and then Isaac turns back around.

"What do you think?" Isaac asks.

"I don't know. They had a dog but no dog and no fence for the dog unless they had one of those electric invisible fences." Hayden answers.

"Yeah," Isaac remarks. "I say we pass." Hayden quickly nods. The boys slowly drive back toward the highway turnoff. As they get ready to come down by the house, a Lexus drives up and into the garage.

Both boys slow down and look. A dog comes from under the steps, and it's a Pit bull. Isaac swallows hard. He had been bitten by a dog when he was younger, which left a bad taste in his mouth over the situation. It was a small dog, but since then, he never owned a dog, even though his brother wanted one.

"Good thing we didn't stop," Hayden said. Isaac nods. The man gets out of the car and opens the trunk. He stops and looks at the boys as they quickly look away and go to the stop sign.

"Right or Left?" Isaac asks. Right was home, but left was the city.

"Let's go home and go to the swimming hole," Hayden suggests. Suddenly, Isaac looks in the rearview mirror, and the man from the Lexus is standing in the middle of the road by his house with a shotgun.

"Holy shit," Isaac yells and turns left and leaves.

"What?" Hayden yells, looking back. "Ah shit. Dude, I told you people don't like anyone coming onto their property in the country."

"Ok. Ok." Isaac yells back. He keeps checking the rearview mirror, and now the man is walking on the highway with the shotgun. "Fuck he's in the middle of the Highway."

"Why did you go this way?" Hayden yells.

"I thought he would chase us, and I didn't want him to know where we lived." Isaac stammers. "I'll just drive to the next town, and we'll walk around and then go back home or go home the back road."

Hayden nods. "Sounds good."

"Is your heart still pounding?" Isaac laughs.

"Not funny dude" Hayden says but then starts laughing. "Probably some old man who got robbed once that's why he got the locksmith to come out."

Both of them laugh as Isaac passes the sign to the next town, which tells them they're 15 miles away.

"There's the town there," Hayden announces.

"Check that book," Isaac tells Hayden. "Wasn't there another house close by that is listed?"

Hayden eyeballs the book and nods. "Yeah should be right before the town on the right."

As they come up to the town, they see a small, well-kept ranch to the right. A truck is leaving the ranch, and Isaac slows down to let him come in front. The truck driver looks about 80; he waves at Isaac, who smiles and waves back.

Hayden eyeballs the home. He looks around. "Secluded. No dogs. Probably no other people living there looking at their age. It's probably their home." Hayden says out loud.

"I wonder how long they're going to be gone?" Isaac asks, slowing down.

"Judging by the way they drive," Hayden begins. "All day."

The couple pulls into town, where the speed limit is posted at 25. They slow their truck down, and so does Isaac. On the right is a small strip mall with a bank and several stores. The couple pull up and park at the Hardware store. Isaac and Hayden follow them inside the store.

The couple grab a cart, and Isaac and Hayden are behind them. Grabbing a cart, the couple continues their loud conversation, as one of them appears to be deaf. "Ernie you get what you need, and I'm going to be looking at the decorations for the yard. Then we have to go to the bank, the Doctors for your check up and then we'll go to the Diner for supper."

"Alright," Ernie replies and slowly pushes the cart. Both boys turn and walk back to the truck.

"They're going to be in there for hours," Hayden replies.

"So, you're game for this?" Isaac asks him excitedly.

"One time. Just once." Hayden tells him.

Isaac smiles and jumps into the truck. "I don't know what treasures we're going to find in their house but maybe something old and valuable we can sell," Isaac tells him.

"Just go before I change my mind," Hayden starts biting his nails.

The man who owns the Van gets out of county jail, and we see him walking towards the towing company.

"Can I help you sir?" the man behind the counter asks.

"Yes, I own the Locksmith Van that was towed last night," the Locksmith says.

"Ah, yes. It's $85, and I have your keys right here." the man says.

The Locksmith pays him, and the guy hands him the keys. "You can go right through there when you pull her out. The gate will be open."

"Thank you," the Locksmith says and walks out the door towards his Van.

The Locksmith is rummaging through the front seat and then goes to the back. As he goes from front to back to front again, he begins to get agitated. He comes back into the office.

"Where is the black notebook?" he yells.

"I don't know what you're talking about sir." The man tells him. The Locksmith looks freaked. He begins to pace.

"There was a black notebook in the front seat of my Van, and now it's gone. It was there yesterday." He yells.

"Sir, we don't go inside the cars. We just hook the cars from underneath and tow them. Possibly the police?"

The man nods and walks back to the Van. He looks around one more time and then looks at the dash and where the video camera is above the radio. He takes a screwdriver from the Van and pops open the dash. He pulls out the camera and watches it. He sees the Van being ransacked by the two boys. He sighs.

He plays the video again and videotapes it with his phone camera. He texts someone and sends them the tape. He then throws the camera on the floor. He pulls out a gun and leans back in the front seat. From inside the office, the worker is on the computer. A gunshot goes off, causing the worker to stop working and look out the window. Blood covers the windows of the Van, staining the inside of the vehicle as well.

The man from the street carrying the shotgun goes back into his house. An email comes across his computer screen. He looks at it.

We are compromised. Stand by for the video. Stand by for instructions.

He sits down, holding the shotgun across his lap. A video comes on where the boys are in the Van. The elderly couple at the Hardware store are looking at their phones and watching the same video. The woman walks over to her husband. "Did you see it?" He nods. "Did we turn on the security system?" The man smiles and nods. "We're fine then." She walks with her husband, placing items in the cart.

The boys park on the side of the house with the truck pointing out so they can leave quickly. They go up to the porch, and Isaac reaches for the key when Hayden knocks on the door.

"What are you doing?" Isaac chews him out.

"What?" Hayden gets defensive. "What if they have grandkids and they're home?"

Isaac thinks and nods. No one answers so Isaac pulls out the key and tries the door. It opens immediately. The alarm doesn't go off, but the elderly man receives a notification. He opens it to see a live video of the boys in his house. He notices his wife across the store looking at her phone, watching the same video. She looks up at him and smiles, and he smiles back.

"No alarm," Isaac whispers.

"Why are we whispering?" Hayden asks. Isaac shrugs. They slowly creep around the house. Several boards squeak as they step on them. The house is well-kept. There are several large antiques around, but nothing that jumps out to them. Suddenly, they hear a click and turn. No one is there.

"What was that?" Isaac asks. Hayden shrugs and goes to the window.

"No one is here," He mouths. Isaac goes to the door and turns it, but it won't open.

"The door is locked," Isaac says. Hayden pushes him and tries the door. It won't open. He tried the window but couldn't get it open either.

He steps back and starts breathing heavily. "Calm down," Isaac says, watching him. "We'll just throw something through the window if we have to. Maybe the back door will open."

Hayden nods nervously and heads to the back door. Suddenly, Hayden stops. "Oh my God," he says out loud. Isaac stops and comes back to where he is. He stops, and his mouth falls open. The two enter the room and it is full of animal heads and a huge oak desk. On top of the desk are several gold bars stacked.

Hayden picks one up and weighs it in his hand. "This is real," Hayden says in disbelief.

"Why would anyone just have these sitting out?" Isaac asks.

Hayden looks at the desk and sees a note. He reads the note. "He's getting ready to buy some land in Montana. He's paying with gold. He probably was putting this out when they decided to go on errands and either forgot or was interrupted by his wife. I don't know, but it looks like he probably set it here to get it ready." Hayden smiles.

"This is our ticket out, dude," Isaac says.

"Oh dude," Hayden looks hesitant, "this is probably his life savings."

"For what?" Isaac stammers. "Hunting? Look at this place. He's a hunter. His farm is probably paid off. He'll be fine."

A sound from another room startles the boys. "Did you hear that?" Hayden asks, putting the gold bar in his pocket.

Isaac goes toward the sound of someone coughing. "It's coming from the basement." He whispers. He starts to turn the handle.

Hayden grabs his hand. "Nothing ever good comes from the basement."

Isaac raises his eyebrows and opens the door. Hayden goes into the kitchen and comes back with a butcher knife. Isaac eyeballs the knife and shakes his head. They turn on the light and look around the area from the top of the stairs.

"I don't hear anything. Let's just go," Hayden is barely audible.

Suddenly, from behind a door, we hear coughing. Isaac walks down the stairway and touches the handle. He looks over at Hayden who shakes his head no. Isaac turns the handle and opens the door. A woman is standing on a stool. Her hands are tied together by a rope that is connected to a pulley from the ceiling. Isaac's mouth falls open.

"Holy shit," Hayden says. The woman sees them.

"Save me."

"We need more rope and turpentine," the elderly lady says at the hardware store.

"Don't forget the acid," the man giggles.

Isaac looks at the rope. "It's on a pulley system of some sort, but it's chained right there," he says, pointing.

"Who are you?" Hayden asks her.

"Sofia, are you ok?" a man's voice yells from the room next door.

Hayden starts for that door but Sofia yells to him. "Don't hurt him. Don't hurt Tom."

"We're not going to hurt you," Isaac tells her.

"The door is locked," Hayden says and sees a small slit with a slider. He moves the slider open and looks into the room. The room is dark, and suddenly, a man's eyes appear. Startled, Hayden jumps back. "Shit. Dude, there is a guy locked in this room."

"Who are you," Tom asks.

"How did you get in there, dude?" Hayden tries the door again.

The elderly couple are now paying for their items.

"Do you need any help to load your car?" the lady at the cash register asks the elderly woman.

"Oh no, dear. We'll manage." and smiles at her. The elderly couple leave, and the elderly man checks his watch constantly.

Isaac tries to lift the girl from the chair to somehow unhook the pulley system, but it doesn't work.

"Run, get help," Sophia tells Isaac. "They're crazy." Isaac goes over by Hayden and Tom.

"We can't get out the front door," Isaac tells Tom.

"How did you get in?" Tom asks.

"We broke in." Hayden tells Tom.

"You broke into the wrong house." Tom tells Hayden.

"The master key!" Hayden reminds Isaac. Isaac smiles and pulls it out. He tries the door that Tom is locked behind, and it opens. Tom comes out. He smells horrible, and the boys take a step back.

"What's the date?" Tom asks and runs to Sofia.

The boys look at each other. "The date?" Hayden smiles. "It's June 6th."

Tom sighs. He turns to them. "What's the year?"

Isaac looks perplexed. "It's 2019."

Tom looks at the ground. He looks at the boys. "We've been stuck here 8 months."

Hayden turns and runs back upstairs. He throws the knife on the couch, picks up a chair and throws it at the window. Nothing happens. He steps back. He looks at the back door. He runs to it. He tries to open it and nothing happens.

"How did you get stuck in here for 8 months?" Isaac asks.

"We stopped and asked for directions," Sofia answers.

"The doors aren't opening," Hayden screams from upstairs. "The windows won't break."

Isaac closes his eyes. He pulls out his cell phone. He goes up the stairs and sees the mail on the small table by the front door. He dials 911.

911 operator

"Yes, I broke into someone's house, and I can't get out, Isaac stammers.

Excuse me?

"I know it sounds crazy. I broke into someone's house, and I can't get out. The doors and windows won't open," Isaac tries to explain.

Where are you at?

Isaac moves around the mail and reads the return address:

"I'm at 1832 Oakridge Lane," Isaac replies. He looks at the next envelope and it has a different address. Then the next three all have different addresses or PO Boxes.

Where are you at? Can you describe the house or the town you're near?

"Yes," Isaac yells. "Yes. I'm on Highway I-95, and I'm one mile from Quincy in a little farmhouse on the right. The house right before you get into town."

Hayden looks at the window and sees the elderly couple drive up. Tom is still trying to get Sofia free but is having no luck. Hayden steps back and looks toward Isaac. "They're back."

"Oh dear. Sounds like you're at Ernie and Claudia's place," the dispatcher remarks. "You're dead."

Isaac steps back, startled by the response. He hears the operator laughing, and she hangs up. Isaac walks over to Hayden and sees the truck. No one is inside. "The operator just hung up on me."

Hayden looks at Isaac, "They had two people in their basement. Who does that?"

"Actually, we have eight people in this house," a man's voice replies. The boys turn around and see the elderly farmer, Ernie, standing there leaning against the wall, sipping a cup of coffee. He puts on a pair of work gloves.

He sighs and continues. "Two downstairs, four upstairs in various areas and two in the barn." He smiles.

Isaac and Hayden exchange looks, and Isaac starts toward Ernie. Ernie pulls out a Taser and tases him. Claudia, his wife, comes from around the corner and hits him over the head with a shovel. She turns and looks at Hayden.

"Sit down, you little fuck," and Hayden immediately sits down. He looks toward the basement stairs and Tom is coming up the stairs. Tom puts his fingers on his mouth to signal Hayden to be quiet.

Just then, Ernie follows Hayden's gaze, walks over, pulls out a gun, and shoots Tom in the chest. Tom falls backward as Sofia screams.

"Shut that damn door Ernie," Claudia yells. Ernie smiles and shuts the door.

Minutes later, Isaac slowly wakes up. He is now sitting in the living room. He looks around the room. His hands are in front of him, and they are handcuffed. He looks at the elderly couple sitting in front of him. They are watching TV.

"What's going on?" Isaac asks.

"Well," Claudia tells him. "We came home and found you and your friend robbing our house. We called the police, who are on their way. A car was driving by and stopped to buy some of my delicious berries when they heard me scream and came to help. I was startled to see you both in my home. The man went to take the gun from your friend but was shot in the process. Then you assaulted his girlfriend and shot her. Their bodies are downstairs."

Ernie turns to Isaac. "Then you got upset with your friend and grabbed the gun away and shot your friend dead. Now you're in a heap of trouble."

Isaac laughs. "No one is going to believe that."

Ernie points at Isaac. "You think they're going to believe a punk like you over an elderly feeble old farmer and his hard-of-hearing wife?"

"I didn't shoot anyone," Isaac reminds them.

"Yet," Claudia tells him. Ernie stands up and takes Isaac by the arm and guides him downstairs.

"Why am I walking like this?" he asks.

"It's my wife's tea. We drugged you." Ernie tells him. Isaac sees Sofia dead on the floor next to Tom, who is also dead. The pulley and chair are gone. The room is full of bags of seeds.

They take Isaac to the next room, where Hayden is sitting on the ground crying. He sees Isaac and cries even harder.

"They made me kill her. I didn't want to. He made me." Hayden cries.

"Now you're going to kill your friend. Put him out of his misery." Ernie puts the gun in Isaac's hand and stands behind him, holding onto his arms and guiding them toward Hayden.

"No, don't shoot me. Please don't shoot me Isaac. I'm your best friend." Hayden cries. Isaac begins to cry, but no matter how much he fights to not shoot Hayden, Ernie's grip is stronger, and he points the gun at Hayden and helps Isaac pull the trigger.

The shot goes off and hits Hayden in the chest. Hayden slides down the wall. Ernie helps Isaac squeeze the trigger again, shooting Hayden in the head. Hayden slumps over dead.

Ernie releases the grip of the gun and steps back. Isaac is crying and looks over at the elderly man. He points the gun at him and tries to pull the trigger. Ernie watches him.

"There were only two bullets in the gun." Ernie tells him and takes the gun away.

"Let's go upstairs. Mama has supper waiting, and we have a lot to discuss." Ernie says, walking up the stairs. He turns to look at Isaac who is just frozen from fear.

"Take a deep breath. The first one is always the hardest. It will get easier with time. You took a chance robbing us. Now, come upstairs and have dinner. I'll teach you how to walk out of hell still intact.

The elderly man climbs the stairs. He turns and looks back down at Isaac. "This is a one-time offer boy." Isaac swallows and looks at the bodies and slowly climbs the stairs.

Chapter 3

A Way out of Hell

Isaac slowly came through the door of the basement. He looked at the front door. He knew it was locked. He knew he was trapped. He heard voices coming from the kitchen. He followed the voices and found the elderly couple in the kitchen. The wife, Claudia, was busy cooking and setting the table. Ernie watched Isaac as he slowly stumbled into the kitchen. Ernie pointed to a chair at the side of the table.

Isaac sat down where he pointed. A plate was there, along with a large glass of milk and utensils. The back door had five locks on it. Ernie sat at the end of the table as Claudia loaded Isaac's plate with food. Then, she sat down at the other end of the table and started saying grace.

Isaac looked at her and then at Ernie, who had his head bowed. "We bow our heads to the Lord when we give thanks," Claudia tells Isaac.

Hearing this, Isaac bows his head as she says grace again. They start eating, and Isaac eyeballs her. "Do you say grace when you kill innocent people also?" Isaac asks her frantically.

"I never killed anyone, dear," Claudia smiles. "You did."

"Your prints are on the gun," Ernie tells Isaac. "Your friend's prints are on the other gun."

Isaac just nods, feeling utterly speechless. "So now what?" He asks, terrified.

"Now you go home," Ernie says. Isaac leans back, surprised by this. He looks at Ernie and then at Claudia, taken back.

"I don't understand." Isaac says.

"You go home, and we'll call you when you're needed." Ernie explains.

"Needed for what?" Isaac asks startled.

"You're the Locksmith now." Ernie explains. Isaac shakes his head no in response frantically.

"I'm leaving this town. I'm out of here!" Isaac explains, and Claudia laughs at him.

Isaac glares back. "No. I'm not going to say anything."

"I am," Ernie tells him.

"What?" Isaac asks.

"Your fingerprints, the bodies, the gun. One phone call. Shall we call now?" Ernie asks and picks up the phone.

"I dare you." Isaac says. Claudia eyeballs Isaac. Ernie dials.

He sounds frantic on his phone call. "Yes, this is Ernie Paulson at 288 Pines Road Exit. We had intruders. They tried to rob Claudia and me. A couple was also here buying fruit. There's blood. They had guns. Thank you."

He hangs up and looks at Isaac. "You're going to be very popular in jail, son."

"You're going to be someone's bitch," Claudia laughs and takes a bite of pot roast. "Who's ready for pie?"

Ernie nods and smiles.

"What's wrong with you people?" Isaac asks.

"Son, if you haven't figured it out yet, we're serial killers." Ernie explains.

"I'll let the police know that when they come," Isaac begins to cry, shaken.

A police car pulls into the driveway. Ernie goes and opens the door. "Hello, Wade," Ernie says.

"Officer, they handcuffed me and made me shoot my best friend. They made him shoot a couple they had chained up in their basement, and they have other bodies all around the house and property. The only thing I'm guilty of is breaking into this hell hole." Isaac explains standing.

Wade scratches his head as he removes his hat. "You don't say?" he says, raising his eyebrows at Claudia. "You're telling me that this elderly couple who I've grown up around is lying to me?

Isaac nods. Wade grins. "Where's the black notebook boy?"

Isaac steps back, startled and looks at Wade, who stares at him. He looks at Ernie and then Claudia. Isaac knows he's trapped. He nods. Wade raises his hands and looks at Claudia. "I'll take two pieces of pie."

Claudia smiles. Ernie nods. Isaac looks at Ernie. "It's under the seat in the truck. Wade nods, and Ernie lets him out of the house. They talk out front, and Wade hands Ernie the notebook. Ernie walks in as Wade leaves.

"You come with me and do a job with me," Ernie says to Isaac.

"What are we doing?" Isaac asks hesitantly.

"We have to bury these people," Ernie says. Isaac follows Ernie, and they grab a wheelbarrow. One by one, they wheelbarrow the three bodies to the back of the barn. In the back of the barn is a row of bathtubs.

One by one Ernie places a body into each bathtub. He points to the box where there are containers of acid. "Pour one of those containers over the body. It's sulfuric acid, but I just call it acid. Go up and down with it. Don't get any on yourself. Always wear gloves." Ernie tells him.

Isaac stands there astonished at what they are about to do but does what he says. He vomits each time he does it. Ernie pays him no attention. Isaac cries as he pours the acid over Hayden.

"How long does this take?" Isaac stammers.

"About two days." Ernie says. "Smells bad; that's why we do it out here."

"How many times have you done it out here?" Isaac asks.

"Son, in this line of work, less questions are best." Ernie taps his shoulders. "Here are your keys. Go home. We'll get in touch when we need you."

"Need me for what?" Isaac asks, reaching down for his keys.

"You're the new Locksmith. Pay attention to when we tell you stuff. You'll last longer. You'll be filled in on a need-to-know basis. Know this. We're watching you now. All of us." Ernie says and walks away.

Isaac slowly pulls the gloves off and walks away from the barn. Cars drive by the highway, unknown to them that three bodies are in the barn dissolving. Isaac sighed and walked to his truck, defeated. Inside the truck laid the black notebook, a set of keys, and a piece of paper with an address on it. He knew what it meant. The locksmith van was at this address.

He shut the truck door, locked it, and looked at himself in his mirror. He started the truck and slowly headed towards his home. As he drove a few miles, he passed the first house they had stopped by earlier in the day, where the man lived with the Lexus. The same man who came into the street and then the highway with the shotgun.

As he drove by, the man was there standing in the yard, raking leaves. He stopped raking and looked right at Isaac as he drove by. Their eyes met, and the man pulled his hand away from the rake, made a gun out of his hands, pointed it at Isaac and pretended to shoot him. Isaac looked away and cried all the way home.

Isaac drove up in the driveway and stared at his house. Everything was the same. He walked into the house slowly, scared that he would find his family murdered or tortured. Instead, they were all sitting in front of the TV.

"Where have you been?" Mama asked.

"Out driving," Isaac barely said.

"Well, the yard looks great," Dad replied. Martin smiled at Isaac, and Isaac nodded and went to his room. Isaac got to the top of the stairs and turned.

He looked down at his parents. His parents and brother. They had always been there for him. What should or could he do now? His mind raced. Should he run to them and tell them the truth about how he had stolen a notebook and was just trying to get out of town by robbing innocent people? Or tell them that he had killed his best friend because he was made to? Would they even believe a word of what he said?

He closed his eyes. What if they were watching him right now? Did they follow him home? Did they know where he lived? How long was he out for? Did they go through his wallet? His address was on his driver's license. These people were smart. They would have thought of that.

What if he talked? Then, they would kill his parents and his little brother. What if he called the police in his town? Would they believe him? Would they believe the other police officer? The bodies were halfway dissolved by now, he thought. His head started to hurt.

What about Hayden? His best friend. His best friend since Kindergarten. The best friend he killed. Wait, he didn't kill him. Ernie made him kill him. But now he was missing, and soon his body would be dissolved. His parents wouldn't have a body to bury. He wondered if Hayden would have shot him if the tables were turned.

Why didn't he just listen to his friends and not go and steal that black notebook? He pulled out the notebook and looked at it. This piece of evil. He went into his room and stared at it. He thought about the book and what it really represented. Then he stared at himself in the mirror, and a light bulb went off in his head.

The 43 houses were not just clients. They were the homes of 43 serial killers. The Locksmith wasn't just a random Locksmith. He was protecting the homes. That was his job. Now, it was Isaac's job. Why? The Locksmith just got pulled over for drinking. He probably went to jail overnight. Maybe it was because he was careless and left the book in the Van.

But he didn't. He didn't know he was going to get arrested. It was an accident. He left it in the Van so the police wouldn't see it. He was probably going to get it when he got out. "Oh my God," Isaac hits his forehead. "He came out and saw it was gone. Isaac had stolen it." Isaac closed his eyes.

He probably had to tell the people he lost the book. Isaac wondered if he was still alive. Isaac went downstairs and saw the newspaper on the table. "Are you done with the paper Dad?" Isaac asked.

"You want to read the paper?" his father asked, shocked. Isaac laughed.

"I do read," Isaac gave his Dad a fake smile. The phone rang, and his Mom went to answer it.

"Yeah, here you go, son," Dad said, and Isaac headed up the stairs.

"Who was it, honey?" Dad asked Mom.

"I don't know. They keep calling but saying nothing. I can hear them on the line breathing," Mom said.

Isaac closed his eyes. He knew who it was.

Dad laughed. "Probably some kids playing a prank," Dad replied.

"Well, I hope it stops soon." Mom replied sternly.

Isaac went upstairs and looked through the paper for the weekly arrests. He found a list of names of people arrested within the last three days. He read them all. A total of 8 people were arrested.

Not many, but their town wasn't the city that had many more arrests.

Isaac went to his computer and started looking at the names and googling them. By the time he got to the 7th name, he found the guy. "Thomas Eugene Fairbanks." Isaac sat back and looked at the guy's picture in the paper. Yeah, that was him. He read his profile. He was single. He lived in the city. He was self-employed. He looked through all his pictures. They were all selfies. Weird. Isaac carefully went through all the pictures, and he found one picture of Thomas with a white van in the background that said "Locksmith."

"Gotcha," he said. This was the guy. All he had to do was go to this guy and apologize, and then he would leave town and never see his family again. That way, they would be safe. "Well, at least I'd get out of this town," he thought.

Isaac heard the phone go off again and heard his Mom say hello several times before hanging up. He knew he had to do something, or else this would be his life. He would either have to stand up to these guys and outsmart them or follow them. His only other option was to run not from fear but to protect his family.

Tomorrow he would find Thomas and talk to him. From there, he would decide what to do next. Isaac went to bed, but he had a restless sleep and woke several times from nightmares.

By the time he woke up in the morning, it felt like he had only gotten 45 minutes of sleep.

He looked at the clock. His brother was loudly coming hardcore up the stairs, and he could hear his Mom talking to someone.

Isaac was stretched, sitting on the edge of his bed, when Martin came barreling into the room. "Hey," Isaac said, "You're supposed to knock."

"Guess what?" Martin announced. "Your friend Hayden ran away from home."

"What?" Isaac asked, perplexed. "What are you talking about?"

"His Mom is here. He left a note. They called the police. She wants to talk to you." Martin said, almost forgetting to come up for air.

Isaac stood up and looked outside. He could see Hayden's Mom's car. He could hear her worried voice. He didn't see any police cars but across the street and up a ways was a car with two guys in it. He had never seen the car before. Could this be someone from the notebook list? Isaac closed his eyes and opened them again, hoping the car would go away, but it didn't.

Isaac put on a t-shirt and headed downstairs. "Oh, Isaac, I was just about to wake you. Mrs. Ryder is here looking for Hayden. You said you were hanging with him yesterday? What time?"

"Yeah, I got up and texted him around 0900-0930 and met him, and we went to the Drive-In and had some burgers and stuff, and then I dropped him off at home around 1030 because he said he didn't feel good." Isaac stammered.

"He didn't feel good?" His Mom looked so concerned. "Was he throwing up?"

"No," Isaac shook his head. Martin was next to him at the door. "I ate the same thing he did, and I felt fine."

"Did he seem stressed or worried?" Mrs. Ryder asked.

Isaac shook his head no. "He said his stomach hurt, so I took him home. He said he was going to lie down. I left. I didn't check on him. I'm sorry. I should have." Isaac replied.

"No, you're fine, honey," Mrs. Ryder assured him. The car up the street started to come toward the house slowly.

Isaac looked at the men in the car, but they made no eye contact and just kept going by. Isaac knew he was getting paranoid. Isaac also knew that somehow, in some way, a note got into Hayden's house, but he didn't know how.

"When did you find the note?" Isaacs's Mom asked. Isaac looked at Mrs. Ryder.

"It was on the table this morning," Mrs. Ryder announced. "We checked his room. His bed was still made. His father took the note to the police station."

"What did the note say," Martin asked.

"Martin!" Isaacs's Mom snapped.

"Sorry," Martin said sadly.

"It's ok," Mrs. Ryder replied. "Something about leaving this town and finding himself in the city.

Isaac turned and sat down in the living room and stared at the table. He heard the ladies talk more, and then Mrs. Ryder left. Isaacs's Mom looked at him. "Are you telling the truth? Did you know he ran away?" she asked.

Isaac shook his head no, and his Mom went into the kitchen, and his Mom went into the kitchen, satisfied with his answer. Isaac stared at the paper and picked it up. He turned the pages a few times, thinking about how the hell they got into Hayden's house. Then it dawned on him. They took his ID from his wallet and the keys to his house.

"That's bold," he thought to himself.

He looked down, and his face suddenly fell. On the fourth page of the paper was a picture of Thomas Eugene Fairbanks. It said that the body of Thomas was found in his Van with a self-inflicted gunshot wound the day he was released from jail for drunk driving.

Isaac covered his hand over his mouth and gasped. He knew it was his fault. He knew that he took his life so he wouldn't have to face the 43. Isaac looked around the room at his Mom, who was busy in the kitchen. His brother was sitting across from him, playing his new game on his Nintendo DS.

"Wouldn't it be cool if we could copy one of these games and sell them to people for less?"

Martin told him. "I'd be a millionaire by the end of the week."

"Yeah," Isaac said, walking up the stairs. Suddenly, he stopped. "What did you say?" he asked Martin.

Martin turned to him. "I said, ' Wouldn't it be cool if we could copy games and sell them for a cheaper price? ' Isaac smiled.

He ran upstairs and grabbed the notebook. He then ran into his father's office to the copy machine. "You want to play games," he said to himself. We can play games." He made six copies of the black notebook. He carefully placed each set into six envelopes. He put the envelopes inside his pants, put the black notebook in his backpack, and ran out the door.

"Stay close to home today," Mom yelled. "I'm worried."

"Ok," Isaac yelled, unsure of what she had asked of him. Isaac got into the truck and headed to Russell's house. Isaac had a plan. Isaac had a way out of hell.

Chapter 4

The Plan Backfires

Isaac banged on Russell's door. His sister answered, surprised to see him. "What are you doing here?" she asked.

Isaac looked at her like she was crazy. "What are you talking about? I always come over."

"Not today. We leave for a vacation in a few hours, remember?" she reminded him.

"Oh my God, I forgot," Isaac said. "Can I just talk to Russell for five minutes, and then I'll leave."

"Make it quick," Russell's dad, Frank, told him.

Isaac smiled and ran up the stairs to Russell's room. He was finishing packing. "Dude, what are you doing here?" Russell asked him.

"I have something to tell you," Isaac begins. "I need you not to talk and just listen. Your dad gave me five minutes," Isaac presumes and shuts Russel's door.

The door opens again, and Russell is sitting on his bed, staring at Isaac. "I told you not to take that book, you idiot. What are you going to do?"

"I don't know. They're everywhere." Isaac replied.

"Dude, you're going to go to prison for this shit," Russell tells him.

"No, I'm not. I'm going to leave town and get a new identity and start over." Isaac tells him.

"Seriously?" Russell asks, surprised by that. He holds up his finger. "I have an idea."

"I'm listening," Isaac tells him.

"That would be a first for you," Russell begins. "You call the FBI and tell them everything. Give them the notebook. Ask for immunity. They'll check it out and clear you, and you'll be in witness protection."

"I won't see my family again," Isaac said.

"You were ready a minute ago not to see them, but at least you'd be alive," Russell tells him.

"Russell!" his mom yells from downstairs.

"Hold on," Russell tells Isaac and goes to the hallway leaving Isaac in his room.

"Are you almost ready?" She yells back. Before he can answer, Isaac gets up, pulls out an envelope from his pants, and places it in Russell's luggage under his clothes. He walks over to Russell as he is yelling he's done back to his mom.

"Have fun at Disneyland, you lucky duck," Isaac says, going down the stairs.

"Are you going to be ok?" Russell asks.

"I'm taking your advice. See you when you get back." Isaac says, saying bye to everyone.

He leaves and heads to Lilly's house. Lilly lives around the corner from Russell. Isaac goes up to the door as he sees Lilly's mom planting flowers.

"Hi Mrs. Turner!" Isaac yells. Mrs. Turner smiles and waves.

"Hi Isaac. Go on in. She's doing Yoga in the living room with her Dad."

Isaac raises his eyebrows and goes into the house. He watches them for a few seconds before they notice them. "Isaac, how are you?" Lilly's father, Terry, asks.

"I'm fine. Can I talk to Lilly for a moment?" Isaac asks.

Terry nods. "Mrs. Ryder called and told us. You kids talk to us if you need to, ok?" Terry tells them both. Lilly nods, and so does Isaac. Lilly grabs Isaac and drags him outside to the pond area.

"What the hell is going on?" she asks.

"I'm in a shit load of trouble." Isaac tells her. She stares at him and takes him to her room.

"Won't your parents get mad if we're up there alone?" Isaac asks as they go up the stairs.

"They're hippies. They would encourage it." Lilly smirks.

Isaac grins but says nothing. He sits on Lilly's bed. This was the first time he had been in her room, so he takes a moment to look around. Her room is bright and colorful. He likes it. "I love your room," he says. Meanwhile, Lily goes behind a folding screen to change out of her yoga clothes and into something more casual.

Isaac takes out an envelope and quickly puts it inside her meditation book on the table. He tells her everything and his plan to go to the FBI, as suggested by Russell. Lilly begins to cry and hugs him.

"You should have never gone to that van. We should have stopped you," Lilly cries.

"Should have, could have, would have," Isaac mumbles. "I still would have done it he tells her. "You know that. It's who I am."

Lilly sits on the bed, and Isaac hugs her while she cries. "I'll come with you," she tells him, but he tells her he has to do it himself. He can't involve them anymore.

He gets up and heads to the door. "I'm going over to Darren's house and then to Ella and Madeline's.

"Ella and Madeline are at the lake swimming today, and Darren is painting with his dad at a job site in the yards." Lilly tells him. He nods and leaves.

Isaac sits in his car and sighs. He looks at himself in the rearview mirror of his car as the same car he saw that morning goes by. He glares at them and suddenly backs his truck up and goes after them.

The car notices he's following them and pulls over to the side. They roll down their window to see what he wants. Isaac drives right next to them. "What is your problem dude? Why are you following me?" Isaac yells.

"What are you talking about kid. You followed us." they say calmly. Isaac closes his eyes.

"I'm sorry. I'm so sorry." Isaac waves and drives on. He hears them yell "nut job" at him, but he continues on.

"I'm losing it," he says out loud. His phone goes off, and he pulls over to answer it. It's his mom.

"Yeah, mom?" he asks.

"Are you ok?" she asks.

"Yes, mom, I'm fine." Isaac tells her.

"Well, I'm just worried. Have you heard from Hayden?" she asks.

"No I haven't." he responds.

"Well, his mom called and said the police can't issue a missing person for 24 hours, and since he left a note, he's more than likely just classified as a runaway. Please come home soon today, honey," Mom pleads him.

"I will. I'm just running to see our group of friends and check with them, and then I'll be home," Isaac tells her and hangs up.

Isaac pulls up to the Lake. He sees the girl's cars parked next to each other. Both their windows are rolled down. Small town. Everyone trusts everyone. He looks at the other cars there. Most of them are families swimming with their kids. He walks over to the edge of the hill and sees the girls bathing in the sun.

Isaac watches them for a moment and heads back to his truck. He stops at each of their cars and puts the envelopes in their cars. In Ella's car, he puts it in her glove compartment and in Madeline's car, he puts it under the stack of laundry she has folded in the front seat.

He goes back into his truck and texts Darren. "Where in the Yards are you at? Have to talk. Just need five minutes, please." He takes off and heads to the Drive-In, but before he can get there, Darren texts him the address. Isaac turns the truck around and heads to the Yards.

The Yards was the low-income part of town. Mostly welfare people. The houses all needed work, but at least they had roofs over their heads. Isaac was glad he didn't live there, but he knew quite a few kids from school who did.

Isaac drove up to the house address Darren had given him. Darren came outside. "Dude, I only got five minutes. My Dad is on a rampage today." Darren told him.

"Why?" Isaac asked.

"I told him last night I wanted to be a priest," Darren said confidently.

"Nice," Isaac said. "He flipped?"

Darren nodded and smiled.

"Why are you smiling then?" Isaac asked.

"Because I told him and the rest of my family all at the same time." Darren explained. "My grandparents came over for dinner along with my Uncle and his family and my Aunt and her family. Everyone was thrilled and happy that I wanted to be a priest. Except for my father."

Isaac laughs and claps his hands. "Wow, that's awesome dude. I'm happy for you." Isaac tells him.

"Yeah," Darren responds. He sighs. "Anyway, my grandparents are already looking at where I should go do my seminary."

"Wow, I guess I will have to call you father soon," Isaac jokes. Darren laughs, and they shake hands.

"What's going on?" Darren asks. Isaac tells him everything. Darren's demeanor changes quickly.

"You have to go to the police immediately," Darren tells him.

Isaac shakes his head. "I'm going to the FBI," he tells him. Darren thinks for a moment and shakes his head.

"You're right," Darren begins. "That's a better idea. They aren't as corrupt as the local police. I'd contact a lawyer too, if I were you. Most of them won't expect money unless they take the case, and if they do, it depends on what they charge. They might want this case for free to make a name for themselves, or they might charge you just a bit because you're under 18. No….wait, don't contact them directly. Do it over a payphone instead."

Isaac nods. He reaches into his pants and pulls out an envelope. "I made a copy of the black notebook. I need you to hold onto this and hide it from everyone. If anything happens to me, give it to the FBI."

Darren looks at Isaacs's face and nods. He takes the envelope.

"Darren, let's go," his father yells.

"I have to go." Darren announces, opening the door of the truck. "I will keep this safe." he adds and leaves. "Keep in touch daily."

Isaac nods and drives away. He sighs in relief as he has given away five of the six envelopes. The sixth one he would put in a safe place for himself. Then he would give the black notebook to the FBI and step back and let them do their magic.

Suddenly, Isaac felt a huge relief like he had found a way out of the hole he had dug himself into. His stomach growled. He drove over to the Drive-In he had been at the day before with Hayden. He would toast Hayden and remember his best friend. He drove to a spot a little away from everyone. He looked at the menu as a car drove on the opposite side of him.

He ordered the same thing he did the day before, leaned back in the truck, and sighed.

He closed his eyes for a moment as the lady on the intercom asked the car next to him what they would like to order. The guy asked for the same exact order that Isaac had just ordered. Isaac opened his eyes and looked over at him. The guy leaned back and smiled at Isaac. The man was sitting in a Lexus. It was the same man from the day before who stood in the street with a shotgun.

"Hi, Isaac," He said with a smile.

Isaac felt sick.

"Hi!" A woman said next to him. Isaac jumped. It was the carhop with his order.

"I didn't mean to startle you," She smiled. "That will be $10.85."

Isaac nodded and handed her $15. "Keep the change," he said quickly.

She smiled broadly. "Thank you sir!" She leaves, and Isaac stares at the man.

"What do you want?" Isaac asks as he watches the waitress get out of range.

"I just came for a burger, onion rings and a large Dr. Pepper." the man says.

"Who are you?" Isaac asks.

"That's not what's important, Isaac. What you need to know is that I know what you are doing." he says point-blank. His demeanor changes, and he is no longer smiling.

"I don't know what you're talking about." Isaac says.

"What was in the envelope you gave your friend?" He asks. Isaac sinks in the truck.

"I saw you give him something. I'll find out what it is. I hope for your sake you didn't make copies of the notebook. That would be a stupid mistake for your friends."

Isaac looks at him. "What are you talking about?"

"Don't act like you don't know we're watching you. We have eyes everywhere. You just don't know where," The man says as the carhop comes to him.

"Oh my goodness, you two ordered the exact same meal. What are the odds?" she says, smiling.

"Imagine that," the man says and hands her a $20. "Keep the change, darling."

"Wow, this is my lucky day," she says, smiling. "You two come back every day." She walks away as the man starts his car.

"I'll be checking on your friends and see what it is in that envelope. I think I'll start with that painter, kid," the man says. "I'll let you know what I find. I'm Grant, by the way. They call me the butcher. Want to guess why?" He smiles as he drives away. As he does, he drops the food out the window onto the pavement.

Isaac starts to shake in his car. "Shit. Shit. Shit." he says out loud.

"You ok honey?" the car hop hears him.

"Yeah, I just dropped some pop on my pants," he says and rolls his windows up. She shrugs and walks away. He watches her and then texts Darren.

Darren, get rid of the envelope. They saw me give it to you. Burn it. Burn it now.

Isaac leans back and sighs. One down. Now, he had to warn the others. If they saw him go from friend to friend's house, they'll put it together that he had made copies and given them out. His plan was backfiring on him. He had to just do it alone and call the FBI and just tell them everything. He had to keep his friends out of it before it was too late.

He looked at his phone. Darren hadn't opened his text yet. "Open it up Darren." Isaac said, screaming at his phone. "I'll just go out to the site and warn you," he said out loud.

He backed out of the parking spot when his phone went off. It was his Dad. "I need you to come home son," Dad explained.

"I have to run one more errand, Dad," Isaac told him.

"I'm not asking you son. I'm telling you to come home now. Your mom is on edge. I don't want her worrying about you." Dad said firmly.

"Fine," Isaac said and hung up. He looked at his phone. "Open it up Darren." Isaac yelled at his phone as he turned to go home.

Isaac got home less than ten minutes later. His mom was looking through the kitchen window and sighed and smiled when she saw him. Isaac waved at her as he pulled onto their property. Darren still hadn't looked at his phone. He was probably busy painting. His father always worked late to get the job done as quick as possible.

Isaac sighed and decided he would just call him. Isaac dialed the number and then leaned back in the seat. The phone rang and rang. Then the phone clicked. "Darren?" Isaac said.

"I'm sorry Darren isn't here anymore. He had a horrible accident. Sorry Isaac. You should have listened to us." (click.) Suddenly the phone went dead. Isaac dropped the phone, held onto the steering wheel, and screamed. But no one heard him. Inside, his mother was cooking; his brother was playing a videogame while Dad read the paper. Isaacs's plan had backfired.

Chapter 5

Crossing Paths With a Serial Killer

Isaac sat at the dinner table, wondering what happened to poor Darren. Was it a joke and just a warning? Was he really dead? If he was, did it happen quickly, and he didn't see it coming or did he see it coming, and was it painful? All the different scenarios went through Isaacs's head.

"Isaac, you hardly touched your spaghetti." Mom said.

Isaac looked at his plate. Normally, he loved this dish, but tonight, it looked like a plate of brains and blood. Isaac vomited on his plate.

"Gnarly," Martin laughed.

"Isaac!" Mom shouted and ran to him.

Dad got up and wet a dishcloth. "I got you kid. He must have gotten whatever bug Hayden got." Isaac shook his head no and let his parents take him up to the bedroom.

His father got him in bed while his mother cleaned him up. He hadn't been tucked into bed since he was 10, but tonight he let them.

"He has no temperature," Mom told Dad.

"It's the stress of what's happening. He'll be fine in the morning. He just needs a good night's rest." Dad consoled her.

"But he hardly ate dinner," Mom seemed very concerned.

"He won't starve from missing one meal honey," Dad told her and turned off the light. "Goodnight son. I'll check on you soon."

Isaac nodded and pretended to go to sleep. He texted Darren but got no response. Isaac closed his eyes and went to sleep. "God, please make this end." Isaac said before he drifted off.

Back at the house, Darren's father looked at Darren's cell phone. "Your friend Isaac sure texts a lot," he said over at Darren.

Darren shrugged. "He's got a lot going on. Can I get my phone back dad?" Darren asked.

"When we're done with this job. We should be finishing up in about an hour." Darren sighed and went back into the kitchen. He opens his lunch box and eats the last half of his sandwich. He then walks back into the opposite room, where his father is, puts his goggles on and his air buds in and goes back to work.

His dad was in a room under a staircase, finishing an area. A man hiding above on the staircase, wearing gloves, reached into his pocket and pulled out a piece of wire. He lowered the wire, and it fell in front of Darren's father's neck. He sees it and looks up as the man twists it, and it's now wrapped around his neck. The man then pulls both of his arms back in a jolting fashion and steps back, raising Darren's father up and choking him. Darren's father drops his paintbrush and begins kicking, but within seconds, he stops. The man continues his grip for another minute, watching for Darren, but Darren is oblivious to what's going on in the other room. The man lets go as Darren's father falls to the ground.

The man then walks down the stairs, removes the wire, and walks into the kitchen, where both men have their lunch pails. He puts the wire into Darren's lunch pail and leaves. He drives off and sends a text: *It's done.*

He waits a few moments and gets a text back: *Make the call and toss the phone.*

He calls 911. The operator comes on and asks him what his emergency is, and he tells them he was walking his dog and heard an argument at the house on 417 Everett Street. He looked through the window because he knew no one was living there and the house was for sale. He saw two painters arguing, and the younger one came from behind, wrapped something around the neck of the older one and choked him. "Operator, I think he's dead," the man tells her.

"Sir, I have an ambulance and an officer on the way. Did you try to intervene in any way?" the operator asks.

"I'm 75 years old," the man tells her.

"I understand sir. Please stay clear of the scene so you don't get hurt, but please stay close by so the officer can interview you," the operator tells him.

The man hangs up and takes the battery out of the phone. He begins to drive as he sees a cop coming up the street with his lights on but no siren. Two more police cars drive by. The man continues driving and goes through a strip mall parking lot. He drives up to Starbucks and orders a drink. He gets his drink and drives by a garbage can. He throws the battery in the garbage can. He continues on to the downtown area. He passes the bridge that connects to the on-ramp of the highway. He slows down. No cars are coming. He rolls down the window and tosses the cell phone into the river. He drives onto the highway out of town.

Isaac awoke suddenly to the sound of the garbage man's truck. He sat up in bed. His stomach growled at him. He was starving. He looked outside and watched as the garbage man slowly came up to their house.

When he was younger, he wanted to be a garbage man. He chuckled at the thought. The garbage man stopped and got out of his truck. He attached the can to the back and pressed the lever on the truck. Isaac watched as the can went up to the top and then tipped over, dropping all the garbage into the truck. The machine shook the can several times, and finally, another bag rolled out into the machine. The lever lowered the can onto the ground and the man detached it and rolled the can almost to the exact spot it had been in. He then pressed the button below the lever, and the machine moved all the garbage to the back of the compactor. The man looked up at Isaac, who smiled at him.

Isaac looked at the clock and texted everyone. As he's getting dressed, Isaac gets several texts from Madeline. He reads them all.

"Have you heard from Hayden?"

"His mom thinks he ran away. That doesn't sound anything like him. Did he say anything to you?"

"The police aren't even looking for him because they said he's a runaway. His parents are freaking out."

"Omg, did you see the news this morning? Darren killed his father! Call me!"

Isaac stepped back in shock. What? Darren killed his father? Isaac knew right away Darren had been set up. He started walking in a circle in his room. He walked over to the window and looked out. "Ok," he thought, "Think. What should you do? How should you call first?" Isaac said quietly in his room.

He knew Madeline was fine. She just texted him. He knew Russell was fine. He was in Disneyland with his family. Isaac texted Lilly and Ella. "Are you guys ok?" He leaned against the dresser. His phone dinged. It was Ella. "Yeah, why?" she texted.

"I'll explain later. Be safe. Watch your surroundings," Isaac texted. Another text came through. It was Lilly.

"I'm fine. At the market. Walking to my car. You ok?" she texted.

Isaac texted the same response to Lilly that he did to Ella. Lilly looked at the text and shrugged. She continued walking towards her car. She listened to her music and smiled as she walked. As she got closer to her car, she saw an elderly couple struggle with their groceries.

She smiled and removed her earbuds. They were pulling a large bag of dog food into the trunk. "Omg," Lilly said, running to them. "Oh, let me help you with that." The woman turned, and it was Claudia. Claudia smiles and says, "Oh, thank you dear. The man inside helped us get it in the cart." Ernie smiles. "Thank goodness you came along." Lilly smiled. "Glad to help," she says, putting her bags on the ground. Claudia and Ernie look around.

"Now," Ernie says, and Claudia pulls out a needle and injects Lilly.

"Ouch," Lilly says and steps back but gets very woozy and Claudia and Ernie grab her. "What was that?" She manages to say before collapsing into Ernie's arms. He and Claudia shove her in the trunk and slam the door. They look around and get into the car, and drive away, leaving her groceries and the basket with the dog food behind.

Isaac goes downstairs and looks at his mom. "Mom, I have something I need to tell you." Isaac takes a deep breath.

"Is she pregnant?" Mom asks.

Martin howls. "Ooooooh, you're going to be a dad."

"No!" Isaac yells. "No one is pregnant." He shakes his head at the thought and walks out the front door as she yells for him to come back. He jumps into his truck and drives toward the police station. As he gets closer, his phone rings, but he doesn't recognize the number, so he declines it. The caller calls back again, and then it hits him. "It's them."

He pulls over and answers the call. He puts it on speaker.

"Hello Isaac."

"Who is this?" Isaac asks.

"You know who it is. But let's get better acquainted. First of all, I can tell I'm on speaker. Is anyone in the car with you?"

It was a woman's voice. Isaac didn't recognize it. "No one is in the truck with me."

"Good. My name is Victoria. I'm in charge. Do you understand what that means Isaac?" Victoria asks.

She sounded sophisticated. Isaac wondered what she looked like or if she was close by and could see him. Isaac looked around. "It means you're the boss." Isaac said.

"Do we have tone in our voice Isaac? I sure hope not." Victoria asks.

Isaac stared at the phone and sighed. He wasn't willing to take a chance and piss off this lady. He didn't know what she was capable of. He knew that she had a network of people working for her or with her. "I'm sorry. I just found out my friend Darren killed his father even though I know he didn't. And the whole thing with Hayden. It's a lot to take in," Isaac explains.

"Oh Isaac, it's going to get a lot messier if you continue driving to the police station." Victoria tells him. Isaac stares at the phone. How did she know? How are they doing all this? Isaac looked around.

He saw a man loading his car. People were just driving by. A couple of people at a bus stop. Random everyday people were doing everyday things. Any one of these people could be one of them.

"We blend in, don't we, Isaac?" Victoria asks.

Isaac knew she was watching him. But which one was she? "Yeah, you do. Are you close by?" Isaac asks.

"I'm watching you now Isaac," Victoria says calmly.

"How did you know I was going to the police department? How did you know any of this? How are you doing this?" Isaac asks with his voice getting angrier and louder as he talks.

"We will talk again when you've calmed down and talk like a civilized person. For now, you will continue with your mundane life. Go to the Drive-In and get a double cheeseburger, large onion rings and a Dr. Pepper. Or go to the Lake and take a fresh swim to clear your head. Maybe to the movies or go bowling, and better yet, go up on the ridge and make a fire pit and watch the stars." Victoria says, laughing.

Isaac turns his phone off, puts his left hand on his mouth and holds in tears. He then cries and slams his fist into the steering wheel several times. He then collected himself. He looked down the road. He could see the police station. It was so close. He also knew they were watching. He took a deep breath.

I have to start thinking like them, he thought to himself. What did they know, and what didn't they know? He turned his truck and went toward the Drive-In. He got there and ordered his usual. As he sat there, he started to think and clear his head.

They knew his routine. They knew all his friends. They knew where he was yesterday, and they knew he gave each of his friend's envelopes. They knew he had made copies of the black notebook and gave it to his friends.

His order arrived, and he paid. He ate a few bites and thought again. What didn't they know? They didn't know if he was alone in the car. That meant the truck didn't have a camera in it. They didn't know he was going to talk to the FBI. They didn't know who he had talked to yet, but they were getting rid of two people he just talked to. Hayden was gone and now Darren had been set up. He was with Hayden, and he was made to kill him and get rid of the body, but not the gun. So that meant the gun meant nothing. It didn't matter that he had fingerprints on the gun because the bodies were all gone.

Isaac smiled. Now, he was thinking like them. He felt more confident. He ate a little more of his meal. He talked to Darren in person, and now Darren was being arrested for killing his father. Isaac knew that Darren was passive and would never do this, so they sabotaged him.

Isaac also knew he texted all his friends and that he had given them envelopes. Lilly knew this. But how did she know all this? How was she keeping tabs on him? Isaac started to think harder. Then he looked around his truck. He looked at his cell phone.

"OMG," he thought. They put a tracker on my truck. Ernie must have or that policeman. What was his name? Wade!

Isaac looked at his phone. He opened it. Inside the battery was a round circle beeping. He carefully put it back together. They put trackers on his phone and his truck. He leaned back. He could toss the phone, but they would know that. He had to make them think he got rid of the phone, and he had to make them think he was at home. Isaac smiled and finished his meal.

"I got you," Isaac thought to himself. "I got you."

Isaac backed out of the parking spot and headed to the mall. As he drove there, he got a text from Ella.

"Out with the boring parents looking at school supplies. Whoohoo. Community college. Everything ok?"

Isaac smiled. "Everything is good. Just checking in."

Isaac sighed as he thought of the position he put himself in but more of what he did to his friends. He had to protect them. They didn't even know the danger they were in. They didn't even

know that all of them had crossed paths with a serial
killer.

Chapter 6

Playing the Game

Isaac parked way in the back of the mall and slowly began walking inside. He felt paranoid, looking around everywhere. He had a thought that somewhere in this mall people were there to take him out. Silly as it sounded, it was quite accurate considering the last few days he had.

His life had changed dramatically. Last year, he was worried about being a target from the school bully when he bumped into him and made him drop his final project, destroying it.

Now, he was walking into the mall, trying to come up with a plan to outwit a serial killer. Well, not just one. Possibly 43 of them. He laughed at the thought of the school bully being the biggest problem he had last year since if he ran into him, that would be the least worry in his life.

The fact that no one knew that Hayden was dead. Well, Russell knew, and Darrin knew. He walked into the Radio Shack. He looked at the phones and grabbed a cheap one. He grabbed two extra batteries and he grabbed a remote-control car. He paid for everything and left. He grabbed an ice cream and went back to his truck.

Another car was parked next to his truck with two people in it and someone in the back seat. Isaac swallowed hard but continued to walk toward his truck. "Don't panic. Don't panic," he whispered to himself.

He opened the passenger door and put the items in it. He then went to his side and slowly opened the door so as not to hit their car door. A woman was sitting in the front seat, and a man was next to her. In the back, it appeared to be a kid. He glanced at her, and she smiled at him.

He flashed a fake smile and got into his truck. Before he could shut the door, he heard her say to the person in the back. "I'm warning you, if you act up in the mall today, this will be the last time we take you here."

A voice in the back whined. "Ok. I'll be good. I promise." Isaac sighs and locks the door and starts his truck as the family gets out. They walk across the parking lot, and the kid turns and looks right at Isaac. Isaac looks at the kid as the kid, who is about 8 years old, holds his fingers up to Isaac like a gun and acts like he shoots him.

Isaacs's mouth falls open. The father sees what the son does and looks at Isaac and mouths, "I'm sorry," while grabbing his son's hand and pulling them down. Isaac puts his hands on his forehead, closes his eyes, and sighs.

Isaac heads home and goes inside. His mom and dad are gone, and his brother Martin is playing a video game. "Are you still playing that?" Isaac asks.

"I love this game." Martin moans. Isaac pulls out the remote-control car and hands it to Martin.

"Here, I got this for you. Play with this for a while," Isaac says.

"Cool!" Martin screams joyfully. "Why are you being so nice to me?"

Isaac shrugs. "I'm older. I should. You're my little brother. I have your back, and hopefully, you have mine."

"What did you do?" Martin asks, grinning.

Isaac grins and shakes his head. "Nothing dude."

"She's pregnant, isn't she?" Martin grins.

Isaac laughs. "She doesn't even exist…. yet."

"Huh?" Martin asks. Isaac laughs and walks into the kitchen.

"Where's mom and dad?" Isaac asks.

"They went to visit Grandma at the nursing home. I didn't want to go because it's depressing and smelly there." Martin says.

Isaac nods. "Yeah, it is. I'll be in the garage and then up in my room if you need me."

Martin plays with the car for a while, then goes back to his video game. Isaac goes into the garage and looks out the side door. No one is there, and he makes sure it's locked. He takes his father's flashlight and lays on his back. He slides under the truck and, using the flashlight, slowly goes under the truck, looking for the tracking device he thinks is on his truck.

He finds nothing that looks obvious. He then opens the new phone he bought and places the battery in it. He goes on the internet and Googles "tracking devices" and "pictures of tracking devices for cars or trucks." He finds pages of pictures. He examines every page.

He goes underneath the truck again and, this time, strikes gold. He finds a small magnetic circle and carefully pulls it off. He walks around the garage and puts it on the back of his father's toolbox, which sits on a shelf collecting dust.

He smiles and sighs. He walks back into the house and goes upstairs. Inside his room, he goes through his list of friends and loads their numbers into the new phone. He then places the old phone on the counter. He sits back on his bed and smiles.

"One step ahead now," he says out loud as he texts the group the same message.

This is Isaac. I'm texting you on a throwaway phone. Don't text me on the other number anymore. I will explain in person. Meet me tonight at the fire pit. At 8 p.m. I will explain all this. Please. I need you guys. It's so important.

Isaac

Isaac leans back as he slowly gets replies from everyone.

"Ok" from Ella

"In Disneyland still," Russell texts. "but I'll be available by Skype."

"See you tonight," says Madeline.

"See you tonight," says Lilly. "Are you ok?"

Isaac texts back to everyone:

See you all tonight. I will explain everything. I'm ok. Skype with us Russell, 8 p.m.

Isaac smiles as he sits up and puts both phones in his pocket.

A man holding Lilly's cell phone looks at the text and hands the phone to the man next to him. The man looks at the phone and then walks away with it. The man holding the phone is wearing a three-piece Armani suit and black leather gloves. The other man is the Butcher. He is wearing long gloves and a black apron.

Across from them, hanging from a chain upside down, is Lilly. She has a gag in her mouth, and she is crying. She is trying to look at them from her standpoint but is having a hard time. The butcher watches her.

He walks over to her, touches her body so it can't sway, and whispers to her. "It will be over in a few moments. You're going to a better place." She cries and shakes her head no. The butcher smiles and nods. "You have no say in this. None of this is your fault. You were just in the wrong place at the wrong time. Actually, you can thank your friend Isaac for getting you involved. But don't worry, your parents will think you are traveling across the country. Plus, you'll see your friend Hayden soon."

Lilly looks serious and cries now that she's realized everything Isaac tried to tell her was true. The butcher smiles and stands up. He kicks her in the face, knocking her out.

The other man looks at him and what he did and holds his hands up, demanding, "Why?" The butcher looks at him and smiles. "It's not her fault she's here. She doesn't deserve any of this. I don't want her to suffer."

The butcher walks over to the table, grabs a syringe, and fills it. He walks over to Lilly and injects her. She kicks for a few moments and her eyes open and roll back. Within seconds, she stops.

He cuts her down and leaves her there on the ground. He takes off the chains and walks over to the trunk of his car and removes the apron and gloves.

The other man looks at his cell phone. "Victoria is not happy," he says to the butcher.

"If Victoria isn't happy, then no one is happy. Someone is going to pay," The butcher replies. He gets into the Lexus and rolls his window down. "Let the dogs out and let them eat. I'll see you at the house tonight."

The man nods. He walks over to the barn and opens the doors wide open. He walks over to a kennel where dogs are barking. He walks inside the kennels, and the dogs, around ten of them, stop barking immediately and sit still. He looks at them. He pulls up a lever, and their cages all open simultaneously. None of them move. They sit there watching him.

"Come!" he says loudly. The dogs immediately come to him and sit in front of him. He looks at each one of them. He looks behind him at Lilly and points at her. "Go eat." The dogs take off running and attack Lilly's body. He walks over to the dogs but stays at a distance and videotapes what the dogs are doing.

"Would have been more fun if she had been alive," he says as he smiles.

Isaac goes downstairs and grabs the paper. He looks for anything on Darren, but nothing is in the paper. He puts on the news and the local news shows the house Darren and his Dad were working on. They show the police taking Darren into the back of a police car. He is shaking his head and looking right into the camera. "I swear I didn't do this," he cries.

They then show a wrapped body being taken into the coroner's car. The reporter says that the son insists he was painting in another room when his father was attacked. But police have found evidence of the murder weapon in the son's lunch box. They are taking the evidence to be dusted for prints. Till then, the son will be kept in the county jail until further investigation. His wife has been notified and had no comment.

Isaac turned off the TV and threw the remote on the table. He places his head into his hands and shakes his head. Martin is sitting on the couch with his videogame in his hand and has seen the whole thing. Martin looks shocked at the TV and then over to Isaac.

"Darren would never kill his Dad," Martin says.

"I know," Isaac remarks.

"He was afraid of him," Martin responds. "I mean, really afraid of him."

Isaac looks at his brother. "What are you talking about?"

Martin puts his game down. He looks at Isaac. "Darren came over last week to drop off that paper assignment you needed, and his father was in the car honking the horn at him. Yelling for him to hurry. I took the paper, and he turned and went back to the van. His father got out and smacked him against the side of his head by his ears, telling him he was useless and worthless. He cowered. He never raised his hand. He just went into the van and looked out the window. Then drove off."

Isaac nodded. He hugged Martin and went into his room. Isaac started to think. Darren might be able to get away with this. Self-defense from years of abuse, he thought to himself. He could be a witness and say it was he who saw it instead of Martin. He nodded. He would do that.

Isaac walked out toward his truck, looked over at the toolbox, and grinned. They wouldn't know where he was. They would think he was at home. He now had freedom. He also thought how smart he was to get a new phone. That way, his friends were safe.

Isaac drove over to Darren's house. Several cars were there, including a police car. He sat in the truck wondering if he should just come back when the front door was open, and the policeman had left. The police looked over at Isaac in his truck and then at Mrs. Thompson, who told the officers, "Oh, that's just one of my son's school friends."

The officer nodded and left. Isaac was surprised they didn't talk to him. Mrs. Thompson told the people in her living room she'd be right back and slowly walked to Isaacs's truck.

Isaac wondered if he should get out? Should he hug her? He sat in the truck instead. He rolled down the window and looked at her. Her arms were folded, and she had been crying. "He would never do this, Mrs. Thompson," Isaac explained.

She nodded. "We got a lawyer. He's in the living room. He told me not to talk to anyone about this." Isaac nodded. She looked at Isaac. "Isaac, I'm going to say this one time, and then I'm going to walk away."

Isaac, perplexed, looked at her. "OK?"

"Get the fuck off my property and stay the fuck away from my son." Mrs. Thompson looked right at Isaac.

Isaacs's eyes widened. She came closer to the truck as Isaac tried to back away from the window out of her reach. She stood on the runner and glared right at him. "Darren told me everything, you little shit. You got him involved with these people and now they set him up. He's going to jail for killing his father, and you and I know he didn't do it. This is all your fault."

Isaac began to stammer. "I'm so sorry, Mrs. Thompson. I'm trying to fix it."

Mrs. Thompson shook her head and stepped down. "I'm fixing it. Hank beat me for years. The hospital has records of my broken bones, black eyes and Darren's broken nose, arm and ribs. The lawyer is going to say he had a fight with his father. He told his father he was leaving to be a priest. His father got mad, and they fought. It got out of hand, and Darren overcame him. After years of abuse, he had enough. A flashback from all the abuse. He killed him. Self-defense. He'll get fewer chargers. He'll be put into solitary, and I'll visit him every week. He'll be out in less than four years. Then we'll move out of this rat hole and start our lives over. But we'll be away from Hank. Away from this town and from the nightmare you threw him in. Goodbye, Isaac. And good luck."

With that, Mrs. Thompson left. She walked over to the garbage can, pulled out a cell phone, and threw it into the garbage can. A man came out of the house. Isaac was guessing his lawyer. He opened the garbage can, took the cell phone out, and put it in a bag. "You can't leave this here, Mary. They're looking for it. I'll take care of it. Go inside."

Mary goes inside, and the lawyer walks over to Isaac. "Here, get rid of this. It's the least you can do after you got him into this nightmare. Like my sister said, get the fuck out of here and don't come back."

Isaac nodded and took the bag and drove off. He drove and drove and drove until he went three towns away. There in the river, he threw the cell phone away. He then slowly drove back to town and home. On the way home, Isaac began thinking about the nightmare he and his friends were in. How he kept thinking he was one step ahead and how he was trying to fix everything. Somehow, things were getting fixed, but not in the way he thought they would.

He thought he was trapped by Ernie and Claudia, but the gun meant nothing because the bodies were gone. Now Darren was going to jail, but he could get out with less time because of the years of abuse he went through that no one knew about. Darren had hidden everything so well. Isaac never went to Darren's house, not even for a sleepover, so he never knew about the abuse. Darren said he fell from the tree in the front yard. Kids always climbed trees. The ribs and nose were explained from a fight. Darren had covered everything well.

Isaac knew he had been coached. But now, this lawyer, his uncle, was willing to let Darren go to jail instead of joining Isaac and helping him tell the police, which meant one thing. These people were powerful and could get to everyone and anyone. People would rather run than deal with them. He was willing to send his nephew to jail instead of facing them and fighting them.

Isaac leaned back in his truck while waiting at the traffic light. Was he covering all his bases? What if they found out he took the tracker off the truck? What if they found out he had a burner phone? What would they do to him?

The car behind him honked. Isaac looked at the light that was now green. Isaac waved, took off, and headed home. He had to be more careful. They could be watching him now. He didn't want any more people to get hurt. Maybe he wasn't as good as he thought he was out playing this game. After all, he was playing with serial killers.

Chapter 7
A Meeting With Destiny

Isaac went inside the house and ran up to his room. He heard his mother tell him dinner was in 20 minutes. He heard his father ask him about Darren. He saw Martin's worried expression, and for the first time, he didn't have any videogame in his hand.

Isaac sat on his bed with his head in his hands and rocked back and forth. His life was a mess. One of his friends was dead, and his other friend's life was ruined. He had put his family and his friends, including himself, in jeopardy.

He stopped rocking and went to his bathroom. He splashed water on his face. He knew what he had to do. He had three options. One he could go to the FBI and pray they didn't know he was doing that. Two, he could leave town and start a new life somewhere- anywhere. Never make contact with his friends and family again. Change his hair color and cut his hair differently. Wear glasses and put colored contacts in his eyes. Or his final choice would be to just go with it. Go and do exactly what Victoria asked him to do for the rest of his life. Those were his options.

He looked at himself in the mirror. He nodded. "Run." Tonight, he would say goodbye to everyone. He would leave the state. He would sell his truck and buy a train ticket or bus ticket and just go somewhere. From there, he would contact the FBI and send them the notebook anonymously. Then everyone would be safe because the FBI wouldn't know he sent it. His friends and family would be ok.

Isaac went downstairs and had dinner with his family. He looked at each one of them long and hard. This was their last dinner together. He wanted to remember them forever this way. He loved his parents and little brother. "I love you guys," Isaac said suddenly. Martin looked concerned.

His father leaned back and smiled and patted him on the back. "Thank you, son. I love you too, Isaac," Dad smiled. Mom looked at him and smiled. "We know you're going through a lot with what happened to Darren and then with Hayden running away. Honey, you know we're always here for you. Just tell us when you need something."

Isaac smiled. He looked at Martin. "Are you ok?" Martin mouthed. Isaac smiled and nodded. Martin smiled and sighed.

Isaac played with Martin on his videogame until it was time to go. He left the house to meet the others at the ridge. He drove slowly through town, passing Hayden's house. He looked over and whispered, "I'm sorry, Hayden. I'll make this right."

Usually, he would pass Darren's house, but instead, he went a different route. He reached the bottom of the hill where the van had sat a few days earlier when this nightmare began. He parked almost in the same spot as if to say, "I got this." He looked up, and the bonfire had already begun. He smiled as he saw the smoke.

He looked over down the road a bit and he could see Lilly's car. She always parked elsewhere, but Isaac shrugged. She must already be up on the ridge, he thought. Isaac got out of the car and climbed the steep hill. He got to the top, out of breath and started brushing himself off.

"Man, that is a steep hill, guys," Isaac said without looking around. "I should have parked where I usually park, but I didn't want to go through the woods alone."

"Are you scared of the dark Isaac?" a woman asks.

Isaac froze. By the fire pit was a woman. About 25 years old, wearing blue jeans and boots. She had a flannel shirt under a white vest. She had long blonde hair pulled back. No one else was there at the fire pit but her and Isaac.

"Victoria?" Isaac asked quietly.

She laughed and shook her head no. "No, Isaac. I'm not Victoria. But she sent me." Isaac looked around and back at the woman. He slowly walked over to her.

She watched his reaction and smiled. "You're a cautious one, Isaac. However, you're not cautious with the way you're handling things. That's why I'm here. You've been stupid Isaac. You upset

Victoria. That was a big mistake. Now you have to pay for it."

Isaac looked at the woman up and down. Isaac was sizing her up. She knew it, too. She got closer, which surprised Isaac. "Do you think you can take me? Is that what's going through your brain? Let me educate you, Isaac." With that, the woman pulls out a knife. Isaac steps back.

The woman hits her right boot against the back of her left boot, and a knife comes out of the boot, and she slices Isaac's leg with it. Isaac immediately falls to the ground. He grabs his shin in agony. The woman pushes him further into the ground, putting her weight on his chest, leaving him immobile. She digs the knife into his side.

"I'm Destiny. We're meeting today because after this, if you don't get it anymore then you get to meet Victoria. That wouldn't be advisable under the circumstances that she's upset right now. The people who meet her when she's upset don't exist anymore afterward. Are you getting the big picture Isaac?"

Isaac nods in agreement. Destiny continues. "Let me explain why she's upset. You took the tracker off your truck. You changed phones and contacted your friends, thinking we wouldn't figure it out. You think you're dealing with amateurs? You, Isaac, are the amateur."

Isaac was shaking like a leaf. He couldn't move. He couldn't scream because no one knew he was there. None of his friends were there. They were supposed to be. Maybe they were all dead. No one would hear him even if he did scream. He closed his eyes.

Destiny hit him in the forehead with the butt of the knife. "Ouch" Isaac said out loud.

"Oh honey," Destiny began. "This is not pain. Let me show you pain." She stood up and grabbed him to help him stand. His leg throbbed. He could feel blood oozing out. He was too scared to move.

Destiny took him down to Lilly's car and opened the trunk. It was dark, he couldn't see, and Destiny knew it. She watched his reaction as he squinted to make out what he was supposed to see. He prayed he wouldn't see another one of his friends, but his prayers weren't going to be answered. "What is that smell?" Isaac asked, grimacing.

Destiny giggled. "That's your friend Lilly. Well, what's left of her." Isaac looked at her in disbelief and shook his head no. Destiny laughed and handed him the knife. "Hold my knife, Isaac," Destiny said to Isaac's shocked expression.

Destiny pulled out a handheld flashlight from her side pocket and flashed it on the inside of the trunk. Isaac looked at the knife, then at Destiny and then at the trunk. He cringed as he turned away and vomited.

Destiny watched him vomit and took the knife away from him. "You had no chance with the knife. Felix is in the woods with a sniper gun pointed at you. He would have shot you if you had tried anything. Thanks, Felix." Destiny smiles and waves.

Nothing is visible in the woods, with how dark it is. Isaac hears someone using a clicker make a clicking noise that echoes through the trees. Isaac, still bent over, looks over in the woods but can't pinpoint where the clicking is coming from. Destiny watches him and grins.

"I like you, Isaac. You think on your feet. You don't panic. You're constantly trying to figure a way out. That's good. That's the way we think." Destiny claps her hands. Isaac looks up at her.

"I'm nothing like you all," Isaac says. "What happened to her? What did you all do?"

Destiny smiles. "She was eaten by a pack of hungry dogs. That's what's left of her. And you are like us. You just haven't figured it out yet. Here's what you're going to do. You're going to take this car and drive it to the address that is written on a piece of paper lying in the front of the seat. You're going to be met by Wolf, who is the man at this address who will dispose of this …mess and then you will come home and go home like nothing happened."

"Till you need me again," Isaac remarks.

Destiny smiles. "You're catching on."

"So, this is what I'm going to do from now on? Dispose of your jobs?" Isaac asks.

Destiny shakes her head no. "No Isaac, you're disposing your mistake. You made the mistake of turning off the tracker, getting the new phone and making copies of the black notebook."

"So, this is my punishment?" Isaac asks.

Destiny again shakes her head no. "No, this is not your punishment. You will get that later. This is us fixing your errors. You should have never made those copies. How many did you make, Isaac?"

Isaac sighs and stands up. He stumbles a bit, feeling woozy. "I made five of them," Isaac says. Destiny thinks and nods. She pulls out her phone.

"He made five copies," Destiny remarks. We hear a woman sigh.

"Take care of it, boys," the woman remarks. We hear a car door slam. Isaac looks, and a black car, well-hidden on the street, opens. He sees two men get out and the figure of a woman in the car. The door shuts, and the light goes out and the car starts and drives right by them.

Destiny smiles and waves but the car doesn't slow down and keeps on going. The windows are all tinted, so Isaac can't see into it. Isaac looks back as the men just walk away through the woods.

"Do you understand what's happening now Isaac?" Destiny asks.

Isaac looks at her. "You're going to kill or set up all my friends." Destiny smiles and claps her hands.

"I like you. You're smart." Destiny giggles.

"That is a punishment," Isaac says. "But it's my fault. Not there's. Please just let me get the envelopes back from them. You don't have to. Let me fix my mistakes."

Destiny walks over to his face. "No, Isaac. You're not in charge. Victoria is. What she says goes. When someone makes a mistake, we fix it as a family. Then we punish the member who makes the mistake."

"This isn't the punishment?" Isaac asks.

Destiny shakes her head no. "This is nothing." She walks over to the woods, and Isaac hears a motorcycle start. She zooms by him and leaves.

Isaac slowly walks over to Lilly's car and gets inside. Inside is an address from a town four towns away. A map sits there, showing Isaac how to get there. Next to the map is the burner phone. Isaac looks at it.

He reads the last message Lilly sends.

Just got a text from Isaac. He canceled the meeting tonight. He can't leave the house. Parents grounded him. He'll be contact tomorrow. Love you all. Lilly

Isaac leans back and starts the car. He looks back at the fire pit burning and sees a man standing there. He can't make the man out, but through the dark shadow, he sees him point to his watch and to the road. Isaac knows he's being watched. He also knows he's being timed. Isaac leaves toward the back roads where the map tells him to go.

He reaches the address by 10:45 p.m. He has driven for a long time. Isaac looks at the junkyard. He knows what's going to happen. It was actually a perfect place to get rid of a car. He's about to press the button when the doors slide open. A man sitting by the office points to the back area, and Isaac waves and drives back there.

Another man waves him in and points to a spot and tells him to stop. He walks over to the car, and Isaac looks up at the enormous machine. He knows what it is. It's going to crush the car.

"Well, are you going to get out of the car, or do you want to be crushed with it?" the man with no teeth asks, chewing on his cigar.

"Sorry," Isaac says, getting out of the car. The man points to an area in the back.

"Stand back there," he bellows, and Isaac follows instructions. Isaac looks at his shirt. His name is sewn in as a nametag. It says: Paul.

"Are you the Wolf?" Isaac asks. The man removes the cigar and bursts out laughing. He shakes his head and points to the man who is now standing against a row of cars. Isaac looks at the man.

He is wearing a suit and tie. He looks like he just walked out of a business meeting and is about to sell Isaac insurance. "I'm The Wolf," the man calmly says.

Isaac eyeballs him up and down. "You look normal," Isaac says out loud.

Both men burst out laughing. "This kid is funny," Paul shakes his head as he presses the button and the claw picks up the car and takes it over to a huge canister and drops it.

"I love this part," the Wolf says. Isaac watches as both men get excited when the compactor squishes the car into a tiny square cube. The claw brings it back out and sets it in front of the three men. Paul looks at the Wolf and smiles. He then nods and walks away.

"Good luck, kid," Paul says and walks away.

Isaac turns to the Wolf and faces him.

"You know kid," the Wolf begins. "You pissed off Victoria. No one does that."

Isaac nods. "I'm sorry," he says, looking at the ground.

The Wolf reaches into his jacket, and Isaac cringes. He notices that and pulls out a pack of cigarettes. He laughs. "Oh, you thought I was pulling out a gun. No," the Wolf explains, shaking his head. "That's too quick. I like things nice and slow. I'm old school like that." He smiles at Isaac.

Isaac looks toward the gate, and the Wolf notices it. He bursts out laughing. "I like you, Isaac," he laughs.

"I'm getting that a lot today, and to be honest, I'm grateful for that," Isaac says.

"Let me show you something," the Wolf guides Isaac to another section of cars, and he looks around. "Where did I put it." He looks and then points to a car. "Ah, over here. I want to show you what I like to do."

They walk to a car, and the Wolf stands next to it. "Isaac, do you know why they call me the Wolf?" he asks. Isaac shakes his head no. The Wolf continues. "I like to hunt things down. I like to take my time. When I get them, I like to kill them slowly. Enjoy the moment. Make it intimate. I am a very thorough man. I clean up after myself. I like things to be perfect. Compact. I guess that's why I became a surgeon." Isaacs's mouth falls open, and the Wolf laughs at his own joke. "Anyway, here's a sample of my work." He opens the trunk, and Isaac steps back.

Inside the trunk is a human compacted into a little square like the car was. Isaac steps back again as he tries to make the person out.

"Do you recognize her? It's your friend Madeline." the Wolf says, admiring his work.

"What?" Isaac can barely stammer. He shakes his head no. The Wolf looks at him and nods his head yes.

"They brought her to my cabin, and I let her have a 15-minute head start. I believe in being a fair sport about hunting. I tracked her down. I shot her in the back of the calf. Right about here." The Wolf demonstrates on his calf where he shot her. Isaac falls to the ground, to his knees, crying.

"Then," the Wolf continues, "She got right back up and stumbled about another 20 feet, and I caught her and gutted her." He chuckles. "She was a good catch." He smiles at Isaac. "Brought her here and had her compacted, and now she's here."

"Was she still alive?" Isaac cries. "When you compacted her?"

The Wolf looks at him in disbelief. "No, boy. I'm not a monster. I killed her first."

Isaac bawls as Paul, who has been watching, shakes his head and walks away. The Wolf watches him and bends down to Isaac.

"Stop crying Isaac," he tells him. "You're making a scene. This doesn't look good. Here's the deal. You fucked up. Now your friends are all going to pay the price for your mistake. Man up and own up to it."

"Let me fix it. Let me fix it for the others. Please." Isaac pleads.

The Wolf shakes his head no. "It's a done deal. Victoria made the decision. The family follows her orders to a T."

"Let me talk to her," Isaac begs. The Wolf shakes his head no. "Let me Skype her or text her or talk to her on the phone."

"Sorry Isaac. The marks have been made. We will take care of it. We will get the envelopes back. You will now go back to your truck. Go home. Put the tracker back on the truck. Keep holding onto your cell phone. You are now the Locksmith." The Wolf tells him.

Isaac stands up.

"Taxi's here," Paul announces.

The Wolf guides Isaac to the cab. Paul opens and closes the door for Isaac. "You know where to take him," Paul tells the driver, who nods and drives Isaac back to his truck. Isaac says nothing the entire drive. The driver looks at him now and then. Isaac looks at the picture of the driver on the front console with his name, Alex.

Alex notices this and smiles. They get to the truck, and Alex turns around. "I've already been paid, but can I offer you some advice?"

Isaac looks at him and nods.

"Next time you speak to Victoria, thank her for this opportunity she's given you and tell her you're sorry for putting her in this position." Alex unlocks his door.

"Thank her?" Isaac says out loud in disbelief and gets out. The driver locks the door while rolling the window down and looks at Isaac.

"Yeah, thank her," Alex says again. "You think you're the first Locksmith we've had? You think you'll be the last? You think you're the only one that's ever fucked up? You've only met a handful of us. About what? Eight of us? How many names were in that book? 43. When we voted, all of us wanted you dead for making copies of the black notebook. Victoria overruled us. So, thank her for this opportunity."

With that, Alex drove off, leaving Isaac right where it all began.

"You look like you had an interesting night!" Destiny remarked. Isaac turned to see her on her motorcycle. Smiling that smirk of hers. Her beauty was dented by what Isaac knew about her. "Ahh, you look defeated Isaac."

"I hate you," Isaac remarked out loud. Destiny burst out laughing.

"Wow, you have balls," Destiny collects herself. "Now you know how we clean up messes others make. You've seen us clean up your mess and how you had to help. There are still messes to clean up, Isaac. We have two more messes to clean up, and then you're done."

Isaac looks at her. "Then you'll kill me?' He asks.

She shakes her head no. "No, we need you to be the Locksmith. But you'll learn that when you meet Victoria, and she explains what you'll be doing."

"I'm going to meet Victoria? I thought I wasn't going to do that because I pissed her off. Those who meet her die." Isaac says.

"If you meet her when she's pissed, yes. But when you clean up your messes, then she's not pissed. She's happy. Once we help you clean up your last two messes, she won't be pissed anymore, and then you'll meet her," Destiny smiles. She looks up at the fire pit. "I understand why you kids come here and stand up there. You must feel invincible. Oh, to be young again." Destiny smiles.

"You said this wasn't the punishment, right?" Isaac asks. Destiny nods. "Finding out my friends are killed because of me over a mistake I made is punishment enough, don't you think?" Destiny raises her eyebrows. Isaac looks around and screams. "I'm punished enough, don't you think?"

"Who are you talking to?" Destiny asks him.

"To whomever is out in the woods here," Isaac points out. Destiny gets on her motorcycle and starts it.

"No one is here but you and me. Our meeting is over, Isaac. Keep your phone close always. I enjoyed our first date," Destiny smiles and drives away.

Isaac stares at her and walks to his truck. He gets in, feeling the dry, crusted blood on his leg. He had a date with Destiny, he thought. "I hate that woman," he said out loud and started his truck and headed home.

Chapter 8

Clean Up

Isaac walked into the garage and looked under the cabinet. The toolbox was gone. He stood up in panic. The door opened, and his father walked in, screaming.

"Where the hell have you been all night?" Dad screamed. His mother was directly behind him.

"Look at you! We were worried sick. We almost called the police." she cried, looking at him up and down.

"I'm fine," Isaac pointed to the empty spot where the toolbox was. "Where is the toolbox?"

"Isaac, we demand an explanation," Dad raised his voice. Martin stood at the kitchen door, watching the drama. Isaac looked over at him. He looked stressed.

"I went to the ridge and got a flat tire. I went to change it and slipped. I hit my head and scraped my leg on a rock and passed out or something. I woke up and then came home. I'm sorry," Isaac replied.

"Why didn't you call?" Mom asked.

"I passed out. I just wanted to come home." Isaac explained. "I didn't even think of calling. I'm sorry. I don't know why I didn't."

"You might have a concussion," Dad said, turning to Mom and then whispering. "This is going to cost a lot out of pocket." Mom pushes him to the side, rolling her eyes.

"Well, I'm glad you're ok because with everything going on my mind was racing," Mom explained.

"The neighbor…John has the toolbox. He's working on something and needed some tools," Dad said, moving his arms around.

Mom bent down and looked at Isaacs's shin. "You need stitches," she explained. "We should take him to the Doctor."

Isaac looks at his Dad's worried look. "No," Isaac says, shaking his head. "I never threw up. If you have a concussion, you will throw up. I never did."

Dad nods and sighs. He looks down at his shin. "Well, that needs to be cleaned up. Let me get some stuff. Martin get the first aid kit and some wash clothes from the hallway closet." Dad instructed. Martin nodded and darted off.

"I'm fine, Mom. I'll be right back." Isaac said and went to the neighbors. He walked into the garage and saw the tool chest on the ground. He saw John working on the dishwasher he pulled into the garage from the kitchen. Isaac reached in, grabbed the tracker and walked out of the garage without John even seeing him. It was that easy.

Isaac went to his truck and went underneath it while Martin watched him. Isaac came back up and looked at Martin. "Where were you really?" Martin asked, concerned.

"Burying a body," Isaac said bluntly.

"Fine if you don't want to tell me," Martin said, walking away mad. Isaac looked at him, and a realization came over him. No one cared. No one believed him. He could walk up to his parents and tell them everything, and they would not believe what he said. Hell, he just walked into his neighbor's garage in broad daylight and took something out of a toolbox, and he didn't notice it. The other day, cars drove by a highway while Ernie and himself had taken three bodies to the barn in a wheelbarrow and no one pulled over to ask what they were doing. No one called the police. People just didn't care.

Isaac sat down at the kitchen table as Dad and Mom attended to his wounds. Martin eyeballed him across the table. "I'm fine, you guys, honestly," Isaac reassured them.

Dad nodded as Mom put the bandage on his shin. "It looks deep," Mom told them both. Dad looked at Isaac, hoping he would back him up. Isaac winked at Dad.

"Just think when I get married and have kids, the story I'll be able to tell them of the scar on my shin that didn't get stitches." Isaac laughs. Mom shakes her head and takes the washcloths to the garage, where the washing machine is.

Dad stood up and looked at the boys. "I'm taking your Mom out for coffee to calm both of us down. You two stay home." He points at Isaac. "You go up to your room and get some sleep." He then points at Martin. "You keep an eye on your brother. If you see him vomit, call me on the cell immediately."

"I just watch him?" Martin asked, uninterested.

"You can play your videogame in his room," Dad started, "with the volume off and for two hours."

"Two hours!" Martin whined.

"I'm not worth two hours?" Isaac laughed. He looked at his dad. "Dad, I'm fine. Honestly."

Dad eyeballed him and started for the door. "I can't wait for you to have kids and have this conversation with them."

Isaac burst out laughing. He walked over to the stairway and sat down as he heard the car door slam. He looked at Martin. "I'm fine. Go play." and motioned him away.

Isaac sat on the stairs, wondering what would happen to his last two friends. Hayden had been shot. Darren was in prison. Lilly got eaten by dogs.

Madeline was hunted down like a dog. Russell was safe in Disneyland with his parents, but eventually, he would come back. That left Ella. Isaac closed his eyes.

"Your friend Darren is on TV," Martin tells Isaac. Isaac jumps up and went into the living room. He sat down on the sofa as Martin sat next to him. It shows Darren being escorted out of the courtroom. "He got 2 years," Martin tells him. Isaac sighs.

Two years is better than being dead, he thinks. He watches as Darren is escorted into the elevator. As it closes, Isaac's mouth opens. In the elevator is the police officer Wade from the elderly house. Isaac puts his hands over his mouth.

"OMG," Isaac explains. "Did you see that guy?"

Martin looks at the TV. "Which one?" he asks confused.

"Oh God. Oh God. He's dead. He's dead." Isaac paces around the house.

"You're scaring me again, Isaac. What is wrong with you?" Martin yells.

"I fucked up Martin. Big time." Isaac cries out. Isaac runs to his room with Martin following him.

"Isaac talk to me. I'm your brother. I can help," Martin tells him.

"I broke into a house. With Hayden. It was owned by a serial killer. He had me kill Hayden. He put a gun in my hand after drugging me and made me shoot him. Then he got rid of the bodies. He made me help. Now, everyone who knows me is dying because I stole their book from them. The book had a list of names and addresses of all the other serial killers. I made copies and sent them to my friends to protect me, and now they found out, and they're framing them and killing them." Isaac blurted out everything.

"Are you on drugs?" Martin asked.

"Get out!" Isaac screams.

"Ok. Ok. I believe you. Geez. This is messed up. You have to tell Mom and Dad," Martin tells him.

Isaac stands up, flaying his arms. "Tell Mom and Dad? Really! That's the best you got? What the hell is Mom and Dad going to do to an army of serial killers? Is Mom going to make them pot roast or bake them a pie? What is Dad going to do? Read the paper to them?"

Martin starts to cry and shrugs his shoulders. "I don't know. They told us to always tell them when we're in trouble."

Isaac smiles. "Dude I'm sorry. Lack of sleep. Thanks, bro. I got this."

Martin nods and leaves as Isaac lays back on his bed and closes his eyes. If only life was that simple. They already had the black book. But they needed the copies. They needed everyone who knew about the copies gone. This is why the Locksmith killed himself. He had lost the black book. He knew Victoria would be upset and punish him. Isaac also knew that in the end, he would be killed. First, they had to clean up his mess. The punishment would be his death.

Isaac sighed and sat down and wrote a note to his parents and one to his brother. He folded them both and put them in envelopes. He put the last copy of the list into Mom and Dad's envelope before sealing both of them. He hid both envelopes in the underwear drawer where he knew eventually his mom would find them.

Isaac looked at his reflection. He had one more option. Meet them at their own game. What if he took one or more of them out? He had all their addresses. What if he took one or more of them out, which would give him more time? This would give him more edge. He'd finally have the upper hand again. He grabbed the book. They were so concerned about this book but just handed it back to him.

It was like some sick, twisted mind game. He had already given them the book back but somehow found out he made copies. "Why did I make copies?" he thought to himself, leaning back on his bed and resting his arm over his face.

He thought of searching all the names on the list. Finding out exactly where each house was and then hitting the easiest target. Then, all of them would be searching for the person who did it. This would give him more time to get to the FBI. He still had a copy of the list. That would be enough to get a warrant going.

While the FBI looked into it, maybe his family could get into witness protection. They could all be moved out of state and start over. They would give Dad a new job. Martin would adjust to a new school. Isaac would help him. He would go to college and show Mom and Dad he was mature. They would be out of this hell hole of a town, and he would have gotten them out of the situation by using common sense.

He pulled Mom and Dad's envelope out of the drawer and made another copy of the list. He put the envelope and list back into the envelope and then back into the drawer. He examined all the addresses. He didn't know where half of these addresses were. He went back into his Dad's office and went through his drawer. He knew his Dad had several maps of the state. He found one and started going through the addresses one by one. The ones he couldn't find he googled on the internet. Most of them were in the city.

The others were in outer towns and on huge properties. They were on the outside of the city but all around the city.

He thought for a moment. All of the outer areas were on land. Huge parcels of land. "My God," he came to the realization. "That's where they're burying all the bodies."

These were all serial killers, so they had to bring all their bodies somewhere. That's why the elderly couple lived on a farm outside the city. They bring the bodies there and then to the junkyard. Who knows what these other addresses were? He knew one thing for sure. Just like the farmer and the junkyard, they had amazing security.

He sighed. He was back to square one. There was no way to hit these people. They would see it coming in a heartbeat. If he hit someone in the city there were hundreds of eyes on him. People driving by, looking out their apartment windows or businesses. He admitted defeat.

He laid down and just waited for his fate. He couldn't text the others because then the so-called family would know. He couldn't go to their house or to the police because he had a tracker. He could walk to the police station, but which cop was with them and which one wasn't? He was screwed, and he knew it.

He sat down and stared at himself in his mirror. Suddenly, a text came through. "Can you Skype?" It was from Russell. Isaac sighed and wrote, "Yes."

Within seconds, he was looking at Russell, possibly for the last time.

"Dude what happened to you last night? Thought we were going to go to the fire pit?" Russell asked.

"Where are you?" Isaac asked, trying to make out the background.

"I'm in the lobby of the hotel. See, here's Goofy," Russell smiles, standing by the statue.

"I need you to do something for me," Isaac said.

"Alright," Russell remarks. "Name it."

"That envelope I gave you. Destroy it. Don't open it. Don't read it. Just throw it away so no one sees it. Better yet, just burn it, but don't read it Russell. Can you do that for me right now?" Isaac pleads.

"You mean the envelope that has the list of 43 houses and where they are?" Russell asks and laughs.

"Oh my God you didn't?" Isaac falls onto the bed.

"Yeah I opened it right away. What is this all about? And why can't I get a hold of anyone else?" Russell asks. "Hold on, I'm going outside. Too many kids in here screaming."

"Where are you going? Stay where people can see you," Isaac pleads again.

"Dude, I'm in the parking lot. It's all good. No one…." Russell begins and is hit by a car.

"RUSSELL!" Isaac screams. The phone flips several times. We see only the road. The phone lands face u, and Isaac hears multiple people screaming while running to Russell.

Someone just got hit by a car.

OMG, it was a kid.

Call an ambulance.

Here comes security.

OMG, I didn't see him. He was right in the middle of the street with a cell phone. OMG. Is he ok?

Someone begin CPR.

Did you call an ambulance?

Here's his cell phone.

Someone picks up the cell phone and looks into it. It was a man Isaac had never seen before. He looks into the camera as Isaac stares at him. He smiles. "Hi, Isaac. That was fun, wasn't it? I don't think he's going to make it." The man looks back at everyone. "I found his cell phone. Is he ok?" the man asks frantically.

An officer shakes his head. The man looks back at Isaac. "Oh dear, that's terrible," he laughs and hangs up.

Isaac sits down on the bed and shakes his head. He buries his head into his pillow and screams. Before he knew it he was fast asleep.

Isaac suddenly wakes up to the sound of voices downstairs. He puts on sweats and a T-shirt and goes to the top of the stairs. At the front door is two police officers. His mom and little brother are standing there. He glances at the clock and knows his father is probably at work.

"Mom, everything ok?" Isaac calls down.

"Are you Isaac Rigley?" one of the officers asks.

Before he can answer his Mom steps closer to the officer. "I want to know what this is all about."

"Mrs. Rigley, we just want to talk to your son about the disappearance and sudden death of several of his friends," the other officer replies. "May we come in?"

"Several deaths?" Mom steps back. "Isaac, did you know about this?"

Isaac quickly shakes his head. "Who died?" Isaac asks innocently.

Mom guides the officers in, to Isaacs's disappointment, and they sit down in the living room across from Isaac. Isaac sits on the couch, and his brother Martin sits next to him. Mom sits on the opposite side of him.

"Martin, why don't you go upstairs," Mom suggests.

"No, I'm sitting with my brother," Martin nods at Isaac.

Isaac never realized just how much he loved his little brother. "It's ok buddy. I'm ok." Isaac says. "Go out and ride your bike or something. Go outside in the fresh air."

One of the officers introduces himself. "I'm Officer Lucas Swan, and this is Officer Aaron Whitley. We're here because two of your friends have been reported as runaways. Hayden Ryder and Lilly Turner. Did you know about this?"

"I heard that Hayden had run away. I didn't know about Lilly," Isaac says. He keeps direct eye contact with the officers, showing no fear.

"When was the last time you talked to Lilly?" Officer Whitley asks him.

Isaac thinks and pulls out his phone. "I texted her the day before to meet us at 8 p.m. at the fire pit up on the ridge where we all hung out. Then I didn't feel too hot, so I canceled and stayed home. I told her I would text her the next day, but I never did. She texted back, ok. She never texted anything about leaving or any problems. She got along with her parents. They were pretty laid back."

"Yeah, I got that opinion too. Couple of hippies," Officer Swan remarks.

"They're really nice people," Mom said. Both officers nod to be polite.

"What about Hayden Ryder?" Officer Swan asks.

"I told his mom that I picked him up three days ago, and we grabbed burgers at the Drive-In, and then his stomach felt queasy, so I dropped him off at home, and I went and did my thing. Then his mom popped over and said he was missing." Isaac explained.

Both officers nodded. "You said several of my friends died," Isaac leans forward. "Who?"

The Officers exchange looks. "Russell Freeman was killed this morning in the Disneyland parking lot. He was on his cell phone, and he walked in front of an oncoming car. There was nothing the driver could do."

"Oh my God," Mom exclaimed.

"Jesus," Isaac remarked. "Who was he talking to on the phone?" Isaac tried to look innocent.

"We traced the call, and the carrier said he was calling the High School. Who knows why?" Officer Swan replied. "He was a jock, so maybe to his coach or something. We're checking it out."

Isaac knew that was a lie. He was talking to Russell. That meant one of two things. Either one or both of these officers were lying, and part of the family, or the man cleared his tracks. Isaac just didn't know which one.

Isaac shrugged his shoulders. "I know Darren is in jail. The only other person is Madeline."

The officers nod and walk to the door. "If you hear anything from Madeline, let us know, ok?" Officer Whitney tells Isaac. He nods.

"By the way, your other friend Darren committed suicide last night in his cell. Hung himself with a sheet," Officer Swan told them.

"Sweet Jesus," Mom said as she covered her mouth.

The officers looked at Isaac. He knew they were bad. They were waiting for a reaction. He looked at both of them and nodded. "His mother is going to be distraught. She'll look for revenge." Isaac replied. He watched their reaction.

"How you figure?" Officer Swan asked.

"I always drive down their street to get to the Drive-In. I was driving down and saw all the cars, and she was in the front yard with some man. Turned out it was her brother, who's a lawyer. Her lawyer. She saw me and flagged me down. She blames me," Isaac told the officers. "I don't know why. I get she has to blame someone. She said this was my fault. So, she'll blame me for this also."

"What did you tell her?" Officer Whitney asks.

"Nothing," Isaac replies. "Her brother introduced himself as her lawyer, and he's a smart one. He said that Darren had said something to them, but he didn't say what." Isaac replied.

"Don't worry Isaac," Officer Swan explained. "We'll talk to them." Isaac nodded as the officers got up. Officer Swan walked over to Isaac and whispered into his ear. "Want some advice, Isaac?"

Isaac nodded. "I have this friend. We'll just call her Victoria. She had a similar problem where someone blamed her for something, so she laid low and let others handle it. You lay low and let us handle it. Drive down a different street."

Isaac knew at that moment he had passed the test. He had made a mess, and they cleaned it up. They came back to see if he would crack under pressure and he didn't. He told them about Mrs. Thompson and they would take care of her and her brother.

He also felt uneasy about the sheer mention of Victoria's name. It sent shivers down his spine. He also noticed one thing about all these people he was meeting. They seemed at ease at what they did. Showed no emotion. They had no fear.

The officers left, and Mom and Isaac watched them leave. She grabbed his arm and glared at him. "Do you know anything about this?" she demanded. Martin stared at Isaac.

"Mom I swear," Isaac raised his hand. "I know nothing." Mom nodded and stepped back. She opened a drawer, grabbed a pack of cigarettes and a lighter and headed for the back door.

"When did you start smoking?" Isaac asked.

"When I had you two," she replied. Martin raised his eyebrows. "Don't tell your Dad," and she left out the back door to the side yard.

Isaac had mixed feelings. He had just sent Mrs. Thompson and her brother to their death. He still didn't know what Ella's fate had been. Or even if she was still alive. What he did know is that every day, he was running into more and more of the 43. He just didn't know when and where one of them would pop up. For all he knew, his neighbor John was one.

He felt like a drug addict who was paranoid. He was addicted to the idea of being part of this cult of serial killers. He had already killed one person and sent four of his friends to their deaths. He was actually a serial killer himself. He leaned back and toyed with that idea.

He was now unstoppable. If anyone anywhere ever messed with him, all he had to do was make a call to the family, and they would take care of it. Of course, that means also if they needed him to do something, he would have to help them. The double-edged sword.

He leaned back on the couch. The FBI was only two hours away. If he left now, he could make it. He stood up and walked to his truck. He would miss everyone. Martin stood at the side door, watching him.

"You're leaving, aren't you?" Martin asked.

Isaac nodded. "Don't tell anyone." Isaac grabbed his gym bag, emptied it, and put essential items into the bag. Underwear, socks, T-shirts and jeans. He walked over to his bathroom, grabbed some items and added them to the bag. He zipped it up and swung it over his shoulders.

"Maybe years from now, we can be brothers again. They'll forget about you in years." Martin told him.

Isaac chuckled at the thought. "Ok," he said and left Martin crying.

Isaac sat in his truck and sighed. He put his car in reverse and headed out of the driveway toward the interstate. Then his phone rang. He looked down. He didn't recognize the number.

He declined the call. A few moments later, the phone rang again. It was the same number. He remembered the warning from last time, so he answered it. "Hello," Isaac said.

"Hello Isaac," the woman replied. "It's Victoria. I think it's time we met."

Isaac could feel his heart pound. He just had to make it to the highway. Then, by tomorrow, it would be over. Isaac approached a red light. The ramp was just ahead. Isaac could make out the turnoff.

"I'm right behind you. Can you pull over, dear?" Victoria replied.

Isaac put the phone down and looked in the rearview mirror. A black car with tinted windows sat behind him. The light turned green. Isaac eyeballed the highway ramp just ahead.

He wondered if he should gun it and go for it, but instead, Isaac pulled into the Dairy Queen parking lot and got out of the truck.

He opened the door and walked over to the car door. The mess had been cleaned up. Now was the time for his punishment.

Chapter 9

Victoria

Isaac sat down next to the lady in the back seat. He didn't even look at her. Maybe if he didn't look at her, he could never identify her in a lineup.

"Frank, let's drive around a bit, shall we?" Victoria spoke.

Frank nodded. He didn't say a word. Isaac looked out the window, watching his truck get smaller and smaller.

"Look at me, Isaac," Victoria demanded.

Not wanting to anger her, he turned and looked at her. Victoria was an elegantly dressed older woman, about 60. She had two golden necklaces, several silver and gold bracelets, a Rolex, and several diamonds on her fingers.

"You look like someone's grandma," Isaac said out loud.

Victoria burst out laughing. "I love that." she replied. "I am actually. I have five grandchildren."

Across from Victoria, facing them, were two men in suits. They both wore glasses and said nothing. They just sat there. "Obviously her bodyguards," Isaac thought.

"Is Ella still alive?" Isaac asked.

Victoria looked at her watch. "She should be. Her time is up at 6:30."

Isaacs's eyes got big. "You set a time?" He asked, surprised.

"Oh Dear, everything we do is timed perfectly. Everything just falls into place. Everything must be done in order. I like order," Victoria replied. "You disrupted my order when you took the black ledger."

"I gave it back," Isaac reminded her.

"Yes, you did, after some gentle persuasion," Victoria smiled. Her smile was scary. If Isaac had seen her on the street and bumped into her and apologized, and she smiled, he would think nothing of it. But now, sitting next to her, seeing her smiling, it was pure evil. He felt scared.

"I'm really sorry for what I did," Isaac offered up.

"You're scared, aren't you?" Victoria asked. Victoria seemed excited that he was scared.

Actually, he wanted to just start crying and bolt out the door, but he knew in his heart the door was locked, and he wouldn't get far. He had to stand up to her or at least come across that he was one of them.

Isaac decided it was best not to lie to her. He nodded. "Are you going to kill me now? Is that my punishment?" Isaac asked.

Victoria smiled. "No dear, I need you to fulfill a job in the organization," Victoria replied.

"I thought it was called a family," Isaac asked.

"Family, organization, group, whatever you want to call us. You will be our new Locksmith." Victoria explained. "Since the last one is no longer with us and you were so fascinated with his job, we will teach you what to do. You will be watching all our homes and making sure no one can get to us while we make sure no one will get to you. See how that works so well." She smiles. "Frank go past the park out by the Lake. I love driving by the Lake."

Isaac noticed how nothing mattered to her. How everything was easily manageable. You just figured it out and made it work. As crazy as it seemed. Her locksmith committed suicide, so of course, he would just fit into his place. No big deal.

"I don't get a choice, do I?" Isaac asks.

"No dear you don't," Victoria responded. "You see, I am responsible for 43 families here in this area. I take care of them. When problems arise, I take care of them. Small problems like they no longer love their spouse, or their kids are acting up in school, or they get into trouble with their neighbors or the local police. Then I take care of big problems like the one caused by you and your friend. What was his name? Yes, Hayden."

"Again, I'm very sorry," Isaac explains.

"No bother," Victoria holds her hand up. "When big problems arise, we get together and we offer solutions and vote on them. I can override the decision. For example, when you took the black notebook, we voted to kill you, but when the Locksmith took his own life to avoid punishment from us, we needed someone to take his place. So, I offered a solution to the problem. Everyone agreed to spare you but still punish you." Victoria explained. "Even though I have the power to veto or ok a suggestion, I wanted everyone to think it was there decision. Do you see how that works, Isaac? Do you understand my power?" Isaac started to get more scared. "Oh, look, the Lake. How lovely. Isn't this where all you kids go to swim?"

Isaac looked and nodded. It was creepy and weird how she could go off-subject and seem like nothing they were talking about was a big deal. Like, "I killed your best friend, oh look, there's a McDonalds. Are you hungry?" Isaac thought to himself as he looked at the lake.

"Look, isn't that your friend Ella?" Victoria asked. Isaac leaned forward and saw a boat on the Lake. On the back was a man holding onto Ella. Another boat was across from him, slowly backing toward the other boat. On top of his boat was a cage that he was lowering into the Lake.

"I wonder what's in that cage? "Victoria said. Isaac squinted to make it out. "Oh dear, that looks like a shark," Victoria smiled at Isaac.

Isaacs's mouth fell open. The man cut Ella's arm and pushed her into the water. Isaac noticed that her arms were free, but her legs were still tied when she went in. Both boats leave as the shark goes after Ella. Ella splashes, and although Isaac is sure she is screaming, he can't hear her from where he is. Isaac looks around the lake, hoping that someone will hear her screams and come running out to help her. Isaac leans back, not making a sound.

"No one will come dear, because no one is home. I made sure of that." Victoria smiles. "Another added exposure, I might add. Again, thanks to you."

Isaac watched as the water turned red around her, and the splashing came to an end. Victoria leaned back and smiled. She nodded to the man across from her. He pulled out his cell phone.

"Make the call. It's done." He said and hung up. Isaac had never seen either of these two men before and wasn't sure if they were part of the 43 or just working for them. How big and how far was this family's reach, he thought. But he said nothing.

"There, now everything is fixed," Victoria announced. "Frank drive. Let's go past all Isaacs's friends' houses so he can say goodbye to this life."

Isaac looked at her. "I thought you weren't going to kill me," He asks.

"I'm not," Victoria tells him. "I told you I need a Locksmith. You will be that person and protect us, but you can no longer be a part of this life."

"Won't someone recognize me?" Isaac asks.

"Not when we're done with you," Victoria tells him.

Isaac sinks back into his seat. He looks at Frank who just raises his eyebrows. Isaac was scared to say or ask anything. As they drove by each of his friends' houses, he wondered what life would have for them. They so wanted to leave this town and now all of them were stuck here forever if he had just listened to them.

"How did you get all those people to leave their houses at the same time?" Isaac wondered.

"Easy," Victoria replied. "Up the street is a restaurant. I had sent them all invites to a free lobster bake. Everyone loves free food. I picked the time, and they all showed."

Isaac nodded. "Brilliant," Isaac said aloud.

"Isn't that your brother?" Victoria asks.

Isaac looks and sees Martin riding his bike down the street. Isaac shakes his head no.

"I think it is," Victoria remarks and nods to the man closest to the window.

He rolled down the window and pulled out a long blade. Isaac started forward and heard himself say, "NO." The other man came across to Isaac and shoved him hard into the seat. He pulled with his right hand and pulled his hair back hard. Then, with the left hand held his face tight. "Watch," He said, forcing Isaac to watch.

Isaac watched as the first man sliced his brother's head right off with the blade. He pulled the blade back into the car and Frank continued on down the street as if nothing happened. The man let go and sat back down.

Isaac turned quickly and watched the bike slowly lose balance and fall to the ground with his little brother's body still on it as his head rolled down the street. Isaac opened his mouth, but no sound came out. Tears fell down his face. He looked over at Victoria. She looked at him.

"I don't care about your brother. I don't care about your parents. I don't care about your friends. I only care about my family and protecting them. Do you understand Isaac?" Victoria says bluntly.

Isaac remembers nodding. Victoria looks at Frank. Her demeanor gets soft again. "Frank, darling, take us to the outhouse. Everyone is there. They must all meet Isaac."

Isaac sat back, knowing that watching his brother die was his punishment. He leaned against the car seat and rested his head, wishing it had been him. He couldn't talk or say anything.

Within an hour, they were at a gate. A man came out and looked at the driver, nodded, and opened the gate. There were cars everywhere from a basic Ford Escort to a BMW. The door opened, Frank got out and opened the door for Victoria. Isaac watched as the opposite door opened, and both men got out and grabbed Isaac. They took him, each on one side, and guided him past all the cars. Through the wooded area they passed several men in dark suits who were there to watch the cars and see if anyone drove up to their gathering.

Isaac figured they must all be the drivers of the larger cars. Not everyone had a large car. Several of the cars were beaten up.

They dragged him into an opening where a huge storage unit sat. Isaac looked perplexed. As they walked in, Isaac stood up straighter, starting to gather himself. The building was large like the size of an airplane hangar. It had cement floors, and three gurneys sat positioned in the middle of the room. There was a wall of instruments on the right, and on the left, three beds with IV poles.

All three beds were empty. There was one man on one of the gurneys trying to look around. The other two gurneys were empty. They had hand and foot restraints on them.

Surrounding the gurneys were people. All sorts of people are standing and talking. They all stopped talking when Victoria entered. Everyone looked at Isaac.

He could guess but he was sure there were 43 people standing there in front of him. They all stared at him. No one smiled. It was an icy cold welcome.

"Everyone, this is Isaac" Victoria said in a loud voice. "He is the reason we are meeting tonight."

Isaac looked around the room. Men and women and even a few kids younger than Isaac were there.

Looking around the room, he could be at a restaurant where random people were. All these people looked like random everyday people.

"Say something, dear," Victoria whispered. "You're making this awkward.

"You look like normal people," Isaac said bluntly. Everyone burst out laughing.

"I'm normal," one man said.

"I told you he was funny," Victoria smiled. She raised her hand, and the laughter immediately died down.

"I know some of you are not happy about my decision to not kill him. I respect that. We have the black ledger in our possession. We also have all the copies, including the one he left in his house." Victoria replied as Isaac swallowed hard.

"How did they know?" He thought.

"I want to regain your respect, so I have a compromise," Victoria began. "We will punish Isaac and then make him our Locksmith. He has agreed to a lifetime with us and understands there is no retirement option."

Isaac looked at her. She saw his reaction and walked over to him. "Darling, did you really think that killing your brother was your punishment?" Victoria asked. She looked at Isaac. "Oh, by your reaction, I would say yes, you thought so. No. It wasn't. It was me showing you my power."

Victoria looks around the room. "Cooper?"

"Yes!" a man in the back walks forward. Everyone makes room for him.

"Cooper, take Isaac and introduce him to the chair," Victoria announces. Everyone raises their glasses as Isaac looks around the room.

Cooper walks over to Isaac. "If I were you, I would go along quietly," Cooper whispers. Isaac nods and follows Cooper. They walk past many of the people who show very little emotion as Isaac is led to the gurney and strapped in.

Isaac looks over at the man next to him on the other gurney. Cooper notices this as he finishes.

"Oh, let me introduce you to Jerry. He made the mistake of videotaping a killing. Actually, your friend's death." Cooper snaps his finger as he tries to think of her name. "Yes, Lilly. Anyway, the videotape could have leaked out, so he had to be punished. He had the choice of killing himself or having his tongue removed."

Isaac looks over at Jerry, who smiles and nods with gauze in his mouth. Isaac looks around the room. "What are you going to do to me?" Isaac pleads.

No one talks but Cooper. He pulls out a knife, and Isaac starts to scream as Cooper cuts away all his clothes in front of everyone. "Wait, what?" Isaac is confused.

No one says anything, although one woman winks at Isaac. Isaac lays there naked as Cooper looks around. "Valerie? I need your assistance, please." Cooper announces. No one moves. A woman about 30 walks through the crowd.

She glares at Isaac and puts on gloves as Cooper hands her a catheter. She walks over to Isaac as Cooper straps down his waist so he can't move and then straps him down by the chest. "This is going to hurt," Valerie says as she thrusts the catheter into his penis.

Isaac screams out in pain, which brings enjoyment to everyone in the room. "You didn't wash your hands," Isaac reminds them.

Cooper steps back and laughs. "WE didn't wash our hands, everyone," he announces, and everyone laughs.

Victoria nods, and people begin to disperse, but some take time. Victoria shows Isaac a mirror. "Look at yourself, Isaac. This is the last time you'll look like this."

Isaac looks at the mirror at his reflection and then over at Jerry, who smiles with the bloody gauze in his mouth. "What are you going to do to me?" Isaac asks.

"Oh, I'm just here to supervise. The doctor will be in to operate in a moment." Cooper smiles.

"Doctor?" Isaac asks as Victoria looks at someone behind Isaac. She smiles as Isaac tries to move his head to see who it is. Cooper sees this and puts another strap across the top of his head. "Change all the features. Make him unrecognizable."

"Of course," the man says as Victoria leaves. "See you in six weeks Isaac," she yells as she leaves.

Isaac looks at Cooper. "Six weeks?"

Cooper nods. "You'll be here the entire time. Surgery, recovery, and then instructions. About six weeks." Cooper smiles. "Don't worry, I'll be with you. Oh, have you met my son Hayden? That's the same name as your friend, isn't it?"

Hayden walks up. He's about 14 years old. He looks over Isaacs's face. He looks at the man who has walked next to Isaac and nods. Isaac looks at him.

Overwalks the Butcher. "Hello Isaac, we meet again." the Butcher tells him.

"Oh my God." Isaac cries. "Oh my God." Hayden chuckles.

"Hayden is learning the trade, so he'll be my assistant. Cooper and Valerie will also assist. By trade, I am a Doctor, but I'm also known as the Butcher." he remarks.

Isaac cries. "Oh, I hate it when they do this," Hayden says coldly. "Man up. You'll be fine."

"Hayden," Cooper corrects him.

"Yes, Hayden, show some empathy. He's your patient." The Butcher says to him and then looks at Isaac. "Shall we begin?"

Chapter 10
To the Rescue

Blane peeked up from the line of bushes that he, Shelley, Billi-Jo and Frank were hiding behind. The chain link fence separated them, and the housing community Blane knew their friends were in.

"Look, I know they're in there. We just need to sneak in and look for them," he explained.

Shelley looked around. "It's easier to just drive up and into the community but there are cameras everywhere," she whispered.

"Why are you whispering," Billi-Jo asks. She raises her hand, motioning. "No one can see or hear us."

"Shut up," Frank whispers back. "This was a huge mistake. Why are we even helping them?"

"Yeah, they don't even know we exist," Shelley reminded Blane.

"Look," Blane begins. "They're seniors. They rule the school. We'll rule the school next year we can do something extraordinary. This is that. We're helping our friends."

"We're not friends with them, may I remind you," Frank tells Blane. "We're invisible in school."

"Yeah, we don't belong in any of the clicks," Billi-Jo adds.

"Definitely not with the jocks or proud crowd," Frank announces.

"Or the band geeks or the theater junkies," Shelley chimes in.

"And not the druggies, computer geeks or…." Billi-Jo begins to say before she's cut off.

"I got it." Blane holds his hand up. "But legends are made, not born. If the school hears that several kids went missing, and we found them we would be legends."

They all think and nod. A van drives up and approaches the fence as the four watch. He flashes his lights, and a beam hits and the fence opens. He goes through, and the fence closes. The four exchange looks.

"So, all we need is a car," Shelley sarcastically says. "Well, maybe next year when we're 16 and driving."

Blane leans back, looking defeated. Frank snaps his fingers and brings out his backpack. He opens it and pulls out a flashlight.

"Wow," Billi-Jo shrugs. "Now we just need another one to make it look like a car."

"You've heard of a motorcycle, right?" Frank smirks. Blane snaps his fingers, and the guys high-high-five each other.

"Ok, wait," Shelley interrupts. "Once inside. What's the plan?"

"We split up and look around at the different houses and then meet back at that gate in an hour," Blane says confidently.

"An hour?" Billi-Jo repeats wide-eyed.

"Why would we split up?" Shelley asks. "Haven't you ever seen a scary movie? You never ever split up."

Frank nods. He points at Shelley. "That right there. So true." He adds.

Blane rolls his eyes. "I'm not saying walk into the houses. We're just walking around a housing area. We're looking for our friends. Someone asks that's what we'll say."

"Then when they call the police because we don't live here and walked into a closed community, we can say our friend Blane suggested it because he wants to be relevant in school next year," Billi-Jo smirks, shaking her head.

"We'll say our friends are missing, and we heard they were last seen in this area, and the gate was open when we arrived and we walked in because we've never been here before." Blane explains coldly.

Frank holds up one finger. "One hour. Then I'm going home. I have a paper to write."

They all nod and walk over to the gate. As they do, a small light goes off above their head. A black camera was above them, recording everything they said and did. It moves slightly, watching them as they go to the gate.

Behind the camera stands a group of men and women watching. They are members of the housing community. "Ready to have some fun, everyone?" the man says, smiling and looking around the group.

The others all laugh and nod. "I hope they come by my house," a bald woman says. She pulls out a syringe. "I've been wanting to use this all day."

The others laugh, and they all walk away as the main man watches Frank pull out a flashlight and sigh. The girls cross their fingers. The man smiles while he watches Frank hesitantly flash the gate. The man pushes the button to let the gate open and the kids get excited and run inside as the man pushes the button again to close the gate.

"They're a bit excited," another man comes close to the one who had been standing there.

"Not as excited as we are. What a perfect way to end the day," he says, and both men laugh. "Send a text to everyone about our guests and tell them to prepare if they want to have some fun."

The other man nods and sends out a text:

Four teens on the property. If you want to play, unlock your door. Have fun!

He smiles as he puts his phone away. In each home, text messages, alarms and rings and each of the residents looks at their phones and smiles. Each one unlocks their doors in anticipation.

Chapter 11

A Night to Remember

The four got to the corner of the first block. Houses lined each side. The housing area wasn't huge, but it was confusing. There weren't many houses on each block, but they seemed to face each other and then end with a roundabout.

"These houses are set up weird. Like they could have put more houses on each side, but instead, they put two there and two here and then a roundabout with empty space. A few more houses could have gone there." Frank surveyed the area.

"Well, maybe they'll add more houses later," Billi-Jo explained.

"But look how much land each house has. These lots are bigger than most." Frank motioned.

"Who cares?" Blane said, looking up and down the street. "Maybe it's a new concept and what these people wanted. I mean, at least you can't hear what's happening at your neighbor's house."

They all shrug as Blane points. "You two go down that street, and Shelley and I will take this street. I'll look around at these two homes, and you do those two homes, and then you two do the same, and we'll meet back in the middle of the street there by the light in 15 minutes or less."

"That sounds pretty good," Shelley nods. She starts to walk away when she heard Frank yell.

"What if something happens to one of us? How will we communicate?"

No one answered him and just kept walking. "You'll be fine," Billi-Jo said, shaking her head. "You take the left side, and I'll take the right side.

"These houses and streets are set up so weird," Frank said, walking away. He kept looking back but didn't see anything. "I don't like this. I don't like this at all. Being popular in High School is overrated."

Blane walked over to the first house very slowly, looking around to see if anyone was home. He glanced up at what appeared to be the kitchen. The light was on, but he could see no one there. He could see a small light in the living room, as if someone was watching TV. He headed to the back and slowly opened the gate, hoping not to run into any dogs.

The gate was open, and he went inside quietly like a ninja. He closed the gate and turned to walk away. He heard the gate click. He turned and went back and tried the gate, but it wouldn't open.

"That's not good," he said softly. He turned to go toward the back and looked up at the window and saw a man standing there in the dark watching him. Blane gasped, and the man chuckled.

He backed slowly away and ran back to the gate, pulling on it hard. It would not open or budge. Suddenly, Blane heard growling. He looked behind him, where he was faced by three pit bulls.

"Oh God," he said loudly. "No. No. NO." He looked up at the window, and the man stood there smiling. He had a remote in his hand, and he pressed a button. A red light came on, and the whole backyard lit up.

Blane looked around the yard quickly and saw that there was nowhere for him to run. The three pit bulls turned into 5 pit bulls who had him surrounded. He looked at the fence, but it had a smooth surface, and there was nowhere to grab hold of to jump up and climb. He was a sitting duck.

"I'm sorry. I'm sorry." Blane pleaded with the man at the window. He just smiled and picked up a bell somewhere in the room he was in. He shook the bell, and the dogs started salivating.

Blane started screaming, and within seconds, the pit bulls were making him their dinner. The man continued to laugh at the window.

Across the street, Shelley was also at the side door. The door had no screen on it. Shelley leaned on it to look into the kitchen to see if anybody was home. The door was unlocked and slightly ajar and opened as she leaned. She stepped back a moment and looked around.

"Breaking and entering," she began muttering. "That will look good on a college application." She slowly opened the door and could hear music coming from the basement.

There was no door to the basement, which she found odd. She could see a faint light, and she quickly glanced into the kitchen. No one was there. The TV upstairs was off.

She went into the living room and then also into the two bedrooms. The house looked as if it belonged to an elderly couple. There were pictures of them and a son all over the house.

Pictures of them on vacation. In the backyard. Holidays.

"Do you like the pictures?" a voice said in the darkest part of the living room.

Shelley gasped and took a step back. A light came on, and a man was sitting on a leather rocker. He was about 30, and his hands looked rough. He was wearing a work shirt and jeans, and steel boots. He smiled and slowly got up.

"I'm sorry. This was a mistake," Shelley said as she quickly walked to the back door again. She tried the door handle, but it wouldn't do anything but turn. "I can't seem to get the door open." She told him as he calmly walked over to her.

"You won't be able to," he responded. "I locked it by remote." He held up the remote and shook it in his hands.

"Why? Why would you do that?" Shelley asked him, her voice beginning to shake.

"Why would you walk into a stranger's house?" he asked.

"I was looking for our two friends," she bluntly responded.

"They're not here," the man replied coldly. "But let's check the basement to be sure."

"No, I'll take your word for it. I'll just be off," she added, trying the knob again. It continued to keep turning.

The man calmly walked up to her and stopped at the basement doorway. He continued watching her uneasiness. He seemed to be turned on by it.

"Can you please open the door and I'll be off. I promise never to return," she told him. He laughed a bit and pointed to the downstairs. She shook her head no and began to cry.

Her tears made him very happy. He smiled and put his hand out for her to take. She shook her head, and continued to cry. It was as if she knew the fate that waited for her in the basement.

He slowly walked over to her and put his right arm around her shoulder, and with his left hand, he held onto her left hand. He firmly guided her down the stairs. She cried all the way down.

The downstairs had a huge den. A TV, couch, coffee table and several comfortable side chairs. Then, on the back behind the couch sat a ping pong table and a dartboard.

There were three rooms to the left. The man took her to all three. "This room is where my guests sleep," he said. Inside was a bed and a side table. It was very plain. He opened the closet, and a woman was tied to a chain inside. She had been beaten and was wearing only a nightgown.

When the door opened, she cried and shook. When she saw Shelley and the man, she shook her head no. "Run!" she mouthed at Shelley, but the man's grip was tight on Shelley's hand and shoulder.

"This is Megan. She's been very naughty. I've been teaching her a lesson," the man whispered into Shelley's ear. "She was my housekeeper, and she was told not to snoop around, but she didn't listen. Now she has to be punished."

The man guided Shelley past the second room, which was a bathroom, and put her into the final room. The whole room is empty with the exception of a long table. At the end of the table is a furnace that is equally long in length.

"What is that?" Shelley asks, crying.

"That is where you will lay down and where I will slide you into the furnace, and you will burn to death alive." The man explains calmly. He giggles.

"You're insane," Shelley says angrily, gritting her teeth.

"No, I'm Blaze. This is what I like to do. We all have something we're into. I'm into fire and watching things…..humans burn to death." He laughs as he guides her to the table.

Shelley begins to fight him, but she isn't strong enough, and within moments, she is on the long table and being strapped down by handcuffs under the table with a chain cord.

Shelley begins to scream loudly, but the man just laughs. He goes to the stereo and turns up the music which is playing classical music. He pours himself a glass of wine and brings a chair and a small table to the room. He then leaves again and returns with a camera on a tripod. He sets it up so it captures Shelley and the furnace.

Blaze leaves again and returns with a charcuterie board with cheeses, meats and bread. He then walks over to her, and they make eye contact.

"I'll do anything you want," Shelley pleads.

"I don't want anything," Blaze smiles. "Any last words?" he asks her.

"I hope you burn in hell," Shelley yells at him.

"You first," Blaze replies and he reaches into his pocket and pulls out of bottle of lighter fluid. He squirts it all over her and bends down to her. "That was compassion on my part. You see, it will take you 30 seconds to a minute to pass out from the fire. You will get drowsy and disoriented. You will die from asphyxiation. That takes 5-8 minutes. The pain will only last 15 seconds then everything starts to contract. The soft tissue causes the skin to tear and the fat and muscle to shrink along with the internal organs. They will shrink also." He smiles.

"Why?" Shelley asks.

"Because it's what I love to do," Blaze explains.

"You said WE all have something we're into. What did you mean?" Shelley asks him.

Blaze starts the furnace, and Shelley can feel her body begin to heat up. The pain is excruciating, and she cringes. Blaze smiles. He starts the belt, and she slowly begins to move into the furnace.

"This is a community of serial killers. We all live here. It's a place where we can belong and connect to each other and still do our own weird things we were born to do. I set people on fire. That's why they call me Blaze. Goodbye." Blaze waves, sits down, takes a sip of wine, and then begins to eat some cheese as he listens to Shelley screaming and watches her burn to death inside the furnace. His eyes light up, and he holds his glass up to toast her.

Across the street, Frank knocks on the door of the house he's in front of. He glances over to Billi-Jo, who rolls her eyes at him for doing this. Neither has heard anything that has happened to the others. Billi-Jo sees the open garage door and enters as the front door of the house opens, and Frank is faced by a man and woman who stare at him.

"I'm sorry to bother you both this fine evening but I'm missing two of my friends and was wondering if you saw them?" he asks.

"Please come in," the man says, smiling. The woman smiles and nods and Frank walks into the house as the man smiles and shuts and locks the door.

Billi-Jo walks around the garage and to the back door. The minute she reaches it, the garage door closes very quickly. Faster than most garage doors as she tries to run and go underneath it.

"Shit," she says out loud.

"That isn't very ladylike," a man's voice can be heard. She turns to see a tall man holding a newspaper.

"Who are you?" She asks him.

"I should ask you the same. Who might you be?" the man says firmly.

"I asked you first," she responds, trying to lift the door.

"Obstinate," he responds. "Most young people are today. One of the many problems in this world."

"My name is Billi-Jo, and I want to leave NOW!" she demands and points to the door.

"You're not leaving that way, Billi-Jo," the man calmly replies. "You can come inside and wait for me in the basement. You'll be leaving in a body bag."

Billi-Jo catches her breath at the statement, steps back for a moment, and then begins to look around the garage for something…..anything to defend herself.

"You won't find anything in here to help you Billi-Jo. I made sure of it. So will you kindly go downstairs because if I have to ask you again, I will drag you down the stairs, and it will be a very unpleasant experience," the man says, setting the paper on the worktable.

The man stands over 6 feet tall. He looks about 70 years old and is very intimidating to look at. Billi-Jo, still trying to catch her breath, cannot form a thought and just keeps looking around the room.

"You're having an anxiety attack. You know you're in trouble. You know you're in danger. You know this is your fault, and you can't figure out what to do next," the man says calmly, walking toward her.

Billi-Jo puts her hands on her ears to drown out his voice and begins to cry. He grabs her by the scruff of her neck and then walks her over to the worktable and bashes her head into it. He then kicks her feet out from under her, and she falls to the ground.

He leans down to her. "You caught me in a good mood, so I will give you one last chance to get up and walk by yourself down the stairs to the basement before I lose my temper. You don't want that," he explains.

With all the strength she can muster, she stands up and walks to the steps of the basement. The light is on, and she holds onto the railing and heads down the steps. The man grabs her by the neck and guides her down faster as tears stream down her face.

Downstairs, the entire basement is one large room. It is full of different old equipment Billi-Jo had never seen before. The floor was cement, and on the right-hand side of the room was a stainless steel table next to a sink. There was a drain under the table and a sprayer hooked up to it.

She surveyed the room as the man shut a sliding door at the bottom of the steps, which made the room soundproof. Billi-Jo looked at him and asked, "What is this place?"

"This is where you die Billi-Jo. Slowly." The man smiles.

"Who are you?" Billi-Jo cries.

"Out in the real world, I am a child psychiatrist. It's how I make my living. In here, I am a sadist and serial killer. I'm the Executioner."

Billi-Jo falls to the ground and begins to cry harder. The Executioner smiles and walks over to a table, and points at the item on it. "This is the thumbscrew," he explained. "It will crush your fingers and thumbs." He then walks over to another item in the room.

"This is the rack. I place you in here and tie your hands here and your feet there, and I turn this knob at the end, and it stretches your body. I can dislocate your limbs this way," he explains.

Billi-Jo cries every time the Executioner explains in detail another torture device. He walks over to a cage that has rats inside it. "I could always do the rat torture, which is where I place you in a rack and then place a rat on your chest with a container on top of it, trapping it inside. Then I'd place an iron on top of that. The heat would drive the rat nuts, so he would burrow inside your chest to escape it.

Billi-Jo tries to run to the door. The Executioner doesn't even blink. He just continues with his sadistic tour of the basement. "This is the coffin," the Executioner continues. "You would lay inside, and then when the lid is closed, the knives would pierce your skin, and you would eventually die."

"There are a couple of other items in here, each fun to use. So many choices. Which should I choose?" he asks, looking at her panicked expression.

"Just let me go," Billi-Jo begs.

"I know. I know. You won't tell anyone," he laughs.

Billi-Jo nods and gets on her knees. "Please, I'm begging you. I'm going to High School. I'll be in 12th grade next year. Then, to college. I want to be a nurse," she explains.

He smirks. "High School with their clicks and endless mind games. SAT's. Getting asked to the prom. The money wasted. Picking a college. Moving away. The anxiety there. I'm saving you lots of time, money and stress. The coffin it is," the Executioner points.

Billi-Jo shakes her head, runs to the door, and starts to bang on it, screaming. "Help. Help." She yells, but it falls to deaf ears..

The Executioner comes from behind and turns her quickly. He hits her in the face so hard she falls to the ground. He carries her to the coffin and ties her inside. He then goes to the sink, grabs a glass of water, and returns to her, pouring the water on her face. She comes to and sees that she's already in the box.

Their eyes meet, and he smiles. "I really hate teenagers. Bye Billi-Jo," the Executioner says as he slams the lid shut to her screams.

Across the street Frank sits down at the couch as instructed. He's offered a glass of water by the family as he sips from it. They watch him intently and smile at each other.

"Your both very kind people," Frank tells them.

"I've never been described like that," the woman says, looking at the man. "I don't think I like it."

He nods. "I don't either," he remarks.

Frank looks perplexed. "It was a compliment." Frank looks at the door and back at the couple. His head starts to feel fuzzy, and he blinks several times. "I don't feel so well," he tells them.

"It's because we drugged you dumbass," the woman tells him. "Kids, come help us kill the intruder," the woman yells.

Frank's mouth falls open as he falls on his left side on the couch. He watches, unable to move, as two teens come up and eyeball him.

"So cool," the girl giggles and claps her hands.

"What's the occasion?" the boy asks.

"Well, he just wondered into the neighborhood," the father responds. "Sometimes God just provides."

They all laugh as Frank feels himself being taken downstairs to the basement. He's tied to a chair against the wall. He looks as far as he can behind him, and he can see marks in the walls caused by either bullets or arrows. He looks down and he can see blood stains on the floor.

"Target practice. Who wants to go first?" the father asks.

Both kids yell, "I do. I do." The parents smile and kiss. "You're the best husband in the whole world," the wife tells him.

"I love you too," the husband replies. Each family member grabs a gun and loads it. "Ok, son, your sister went first last time, so you go first, then her. Then your mom and me. Remember to start at the bottom and work your way up. This way, he suffers more," the Dad tells them.

"Please wait. I don't understand," Frank yells.

"I hate it when they beg," the son takes aim. "Cowards." He pulls the trigger, and Frank is shot in the knee.

Within an hour, Frank dies after being shot 16 times. The family looks very proud of themselves as the father tells the kids to put the guns away. "I'll call Blaze and borrow his furnace," the father kisses his wife.

"I'll clean up after you're gone," the wife tells him. "You're the best, honey," she adds.

They kiss.

Chapter 12
The Beginning Of the End

Isaac stood in front of the mirror for the first time, looking at his reflection. "What do you think?" Cooper asks.

Isaac looks at his once straight blonde hair that was now brown and curly. His nose and ears had been reconstructed. All his upper teeth had been removed. Cooper hands him partial dentures. Isaac sighs and puts them into his mouth. His cheeks are swollen, and he touches them.

"That's the Botox. Here are your contacts. You now have green eyes and no longer blue." Cooper instructs him.

Isaac steps back. Instead of the slim body he once had, he has now gained a substantial weight. Cooper sees his reaction. "Don't worry about that. We'll ask Victoria if you can go back to your normal weight. No one in town is going to recognize you like this. Trust me. We made several modifications."

"So I'll stay in town?" Isaac asks.

Cooper nods. "Yes, we got you a nice apartment, and you'll be paid $75 an hour. Your job, as I've told you, is to make sure our homes are safe. You drive past our homes every day, making rounds. It will take you 4 rounds. We'll give you a Van and a gas card. You'll work Monday through Friday from 9-5 like a normal everyday person." Cooper smiles.

"A normal everyday person who is protecting Serial Killer's homes," Isaac asks.

Cooper nods. "You make it sound like it's a hard job. People would die for this job." He steps back, laughing at his own joke. "Die for this job. Get it? People have died for this job."

Isaac rolls his eyes. "What do I do as a Locksmith? What do I do if I see anything?" Isaac asks.

"Don't worry," Cooper points a man over. "Jerry will teach you everything you need to know."

Jerry, the man on the gurney who had his tongue removed, stands next to Isaac and nods his head at Cooper. Jerry smiles at Cooper, who nods at Isaac's appearance and shows him a thumbs up.

"See, Jerry approves," Cooper announces.

"Yay," Isaac mumbles. "So I'm being trained by a man who can't talk?" Isaac asks.

Cooper steps back. "If I were you, I'd be grateful for this opportunity you were given."

"Opportunity?" Isaac asks.

"Yes," Cooper reminds him. "The vote was forty to kill you and three to save you. I was one of the three, by the way. Like in most scenarios the most votes win. But Victoria stepped in, and her vote outweighed all of ours. So you were given this opportunity to live. Don't be so sullen." Cooper steps back and thinks and raises his finger. "Don't look a gift horse in the mouth." He smiles and walks away.

Jerry nods and holds up his thumb again. Isaac looks around at the room he has been in for six weeks. He was never given a mirror to see his reflection. He hadn't been outside for fresh air. He wondered what had happened to his poor parents. They didn't even know where he was. "Oh my God," he thought, "Martin's funeral. He never got to attend."

"Where is my apartment? Do I live alone?" Isaac asks.

Cooper turns and smiles. "We're leaving here today. We're going to one of the main houses. You'll see Victoria again. She'll let you know everything else."

Isaac stands up. Jerry hands him a jacket. "Why do I need a jacket?"

Cooper smiles. "It's fall outside. It's cold."

Isaac sighs and nods. "Of course it is." The men walk outside, and Isaac takes in the fresh air. Cooper watches him and smiles. He nods to Jerry, and the two go to the car. Hayden is in the front seat, and Cooper goes into the driver's seat.

"Give him a moment to let it all soak in," Cooper says to Hayden. Jerry sits in the back as Isaac looks at the car and walks over.

"Do you think he'll accept all this?" Hayden asks.

"You did once you realized it was the right choice." Cooper looks at his son.

"It was the right choice. I have no regrets. But him," Hayden nods at him.

Cooper shrugs. "If he doesn't, he'll have to deal with the whole family." Hayden grins. Cooper looks at him. "No," Cooper says and shakes his head.

"Come on, that would be fun to watch," Hayden says, putting his seatbelt on.

Isaac gets into the car and puts his belt on when Jerry points to it. "What is expected of me?" Isaac asks.

Cooper looks at him through the rearview mirror. "What's expected of you is the same as any job. Loyalty. Stop worrying. We're going to go meet Victoria. She'll explain everything."

Cooper begins to back up, and they take off driving. Cooper's phone goes off, and he looks at it and answers it. "Yes, hello," he begins. "Yes, we're on the way now. Uh-huh. I understand. Thank you, Victoria. See you soon."

Isaac looks at him, and Cooper looks at him. "We're going to make a quick stop," Cooper announces.

"Where?" Hayden asks.

"Sanctioned," Cooper replies. Hayden nods and says nothing. Isaac wonders what that means and looks at Jerry who is no help whatsoever. All he is doing is looking out the window, smiling.

Finally, they reach the town where it all began. Isaac looks around. Nothing has changed. They drive toward the east part of town towards the outer area. A sign ahead tells them to turn left to head back to town. The sign on the right takes them back to where they came from but down a back road route. Ahead of them is the cemetery.

Isaac looks at Cooper, who nods. "It's been sanctioned by Victoria for you to come here. Now, Isaac, this is a one-time thing. You're here to say goodbye to your brother. Do you understand?" Cooper asks.

Isaac nods. Cooper turns and looks at him. "You can only come here this one time. So say everything you need to say now. If they catch you here again, it's considered breaking the rules."

Hayden turns and looks at him. "There are eyes everywhere. Know that." Hayden turns back around as Cooper texts into his phone. He hands the phone to Hayden.

"They'll let me know where he's buried," Cooper says as they slowly go through the area. A text comes in a few moments later and Hayden shows him. Cooper nods, and they continue.

"Right there," Hayden points. "The children's area."

Cooper stops the car and looks around. No one is there. Hayden looks back at Isaac and nods. Isaac gets out of the car, and Cooper shows him the text. It's a plot number and a section number. It also says, "By the tree." Cooper points to the only tree in the area. "Must be over there. I'll give you some time."

Isaac nods and heads over to the tree. Right before he gets there, he finds Martin's grave. A fresh stone is there. Isaac bends down and touches the grave. "I'm sorry, bro. I love you, and I'll always miss you. Forgive me, please. I'll never be able to forgive myself." Isaac says quietly. He rubs his hand across the plate and stands. He looks around. No one is around.

He feels a small breeze go through his body. It was getting colder. Fall was coming. He sighs and walks away back to the car. He walks over to Cooper, who looks at him.

"You good?" Cooper asks.

"Thanks for letting me come here," Isaac says.

"Don't thank me. Thank Victoria." Cooper says and gets into the car. They drive off and continue through town and onto the highway. They go past towns, including the one where the Butcher lived, and Ernie and Claudia lived.

"There's Ernie in the field," Cooper laughs and points. Isaac's eyes widen.

"He's probably burying a body right now," Isaac says out loud. Jerry slaps his legs and nods. Hayden bursts out laughing and so does Cooper.

"You're probably right," Cooper laughs.

They go through the small town and finally hit the big city. They drive into the city, and Isaac's eyes widen as he sees all the magnificent buildings. After ten minutes of driving through the city, Cooper takes several turn-offs and winds up by a lake turn-off. He follows the road around to the opposite side of the lake. He comes across a huge metal gate that is ten feet high. He pushes the button.

May I help you?

"It's Cooper," Cooper announces. The gate opens, and they drive in. They go up a driveway, and around the corner, a log cabin stands. They drive past the cabin to another road which takes them to a big house.

Cooper gets out of the car and stretches. He points to one of the many cars sitting there. "Ah, Roger brought his Roadster. I love that car."

Hayden smiles and heads to the door. Cooper stretches his arms out to the door signifying Isaac to go inside. The four walks through the six-foot-tall steel doors, and Isaac's mouth falls open.

The marble floor offsets the rich dark oak entrance. A large fountain is at the end of the hallway. On the right is a spiraling staircase. On the left is the entrance to the kitchen. Cooper points to an entrance ahead past the fountain. The men walk into an oak room. On the left was a huge fireplace that went from the floor to the ceiling. It was large enough for someone to stand inside of it, and secretly, Isaac wondered if anyone had been put there -considering the people he now worked for.

The room looked like a rustic lodge. It was warm and inviting. Hayden walked past him up to a woman whom Isaac had never met, who was sitting behind a long oak desk. "Grandmother," Hayden said as the woman who was staring at Isaac, took her attention away from him to Hayden.

"Oh my God," Isaac thought, "the whole family were Serial Killer's."

Cooper let out a laugh at his expression, which worried Isaac if he had said that out loud. He had not. Cooper leaned over and whispered to him, "None of us are really related, but we're all family."

Isaac nodded, not saying anything until he was directly asked a question. He looked at Jerry who stood by the window, his hands in front of him, standing politely. He smiled at Hayden as he hugged the woman.

"Have you eaten dear," the lady asked putting all her attention to Hayden.

"Yes, Grandmother, thank you for asking," Hayden politely said. She smiled and started staring at Isaac intently.

Isaac looked around the room. He counted 12 people he had never met before. There were others there he had met as well. Victoria and the Butcher were there, and the man he had seen picked up Russell's phone that fateful day. Plus, Cooper, Hayden and Jerry. That was 18 people in total.

The room was so large he figured another 40 people could easily fit inside. Everyone, with the exception of Jerry and Isaac, was dressed very well off. Isaac was scared to sit or ask to sit or even talk, so he looked over at Cooper.

Cooper smiled and nodded. "You remember Victoria, don't you, Isaac?" Cooper held his hand up to her.

Victoria was sitting on one of the sofas next to two well-dressed men. Dressed elegantly as usual she was sipping a drink. She smiled at Isaac. Isaac nodded and bowed slightly. "Thank you, Victoria. Thank you for letting me say goodbye to my brother."

Victoria smiled broadly and nodded at Cooper who smiled and nodded at Isaac. Victoria sat her drink down. "Thank you, Isaac. That was very polite. But it was Miriam who sanctioned it. Miriam is in charge of all the families who are represented here today."

Isaac looked around the room. He took it that each person here was the head of 43 different sets of

Serial Killers. Twelve people multiplied by the number of families could mean well over 400 Serial Killers. Isaac's eyes widened.

"He's doing math," Miriam laughs. Everyone laughs. "Yes Isaac, and that is just in this state. Could you imagine if we introduced you to everyone?" Everyone laughs.

Isaac smiles and forces a small laugh.

"Let me introduce you to everyone," Victoria stands up and walks over to Isaac,

checking out his face. "The swelling has come down. It will come down more. Put him on a diet. Let him lose this weight. He can be as slim as he was before, couldn't he, Miriam?"

Victoria steps back and looks at him, then at a picture on the desk and nods. "Yes, I don't think anyone will recognize him."

Isaac spoke up. "I could change my name," he offered. Cooper looks at him and smiles.

"We already did," the man in front of him said.

"Yes," Victoria added, "but your offering is a very good gesture. It shows us commitment." The room nods.

The man who spoke looks at Miriam, who nods as he walks over to the desk and places his drink there. He picks up a folder and walks over to Isaac and hands it to him. "This is all your new information. Read it. Memorize it. Then burn it. It should take you less than three days. Know it from top to bottom because we will test you."

Isaac nods and takes it right away. He doesn't open it. Miriam watches him and smiles. "You're very cautious, Isaac or should I say Maverick Henderson." Isaac looked at her.

Isaac thought of the name Maverick. He liked it. He smiled. "I didn't want to offend anyone or do anything wrong. I'm really not sure what I can and cannot do or say," Isaac replied.

Miriam stands up and everyone sits up more as she does. Cooper steps back, as so does Hayden. "This was absolute power," Isaac thought as she walked over to him. Isaac was about 5 foot 8, and this woman was about 5 foot 6, and he was scared to death of her and what she could do in a snap of a finger.

"Just be yourself. Well, your new self," she told him to his face. He nods. "You're still Isaac inside. But now you will learn to become Maverick. If you read about him he is fearless and arrogant. He is slick and smooth. Own it. Become Maverick."

She smiles and walks away. Isaac stood up a little straighter, and for the first time in a long time, he felt more confident. He looks at the man next to him and holds out his hand.

"I'm Maverick Henderson, sir," Isaac tells him.

The man smiles and shakes his hand. "I'm Joshua Paulson. By day, I'm a Doctor, but in my free time, they call me the Butcher."

Isaac slowly goes around introducing himself to everyone.

David Alexander. Plumber. They call me the Candyman.

Eric Isaacs. Bartender. They call me Tombstone.

Rodney Twohatchets. I work in a grocery store. They call me Two Hatchets.

Brad Abrams. I'm a nurse. They call me the Widowmaker.

Cynthia Roberts. Housewife, Mom of three. They call me the Juicer.

Phillip Bender. I work in construction. I'm the Exterminator.

John Jacobson. Dentist. They call me Hunter.

"Sorry about your friend. No offense," Hunter whispers. Isaac nods and touches his shoulder.

Earl. I'm the waiter. They call me Earl. Isaac looks at him for a second, and everyone bursts out laughing. Earl lifts the water pitcher, and John gives Isaac a glass. Isaac smiles and holds up the glass.

I'm Susan Freeman. By day, I'm a massage therapist. They call me the Baker.

Melissa Overton. Teacher by day to third-grade class at Taft Elementary. They call me The Angel of Death.

George Branson. Judge by day. They call me the Executioner.

Captain Michael Malone. Police chief by day. They call me the Claw.

Paul Stewart. Fireman and photographer by day. They call me Psycho.

Everyone steps back, and Isaac nods. "It's a pleasure. I hope to work for you all for many years," he says, hoping it is the right thing to say.

He wanted to say, "You sound like comic book villains." He also wanted to know the things these people did to get their names, but he was sure he would eventually learn the answer.

"To Maverick!" Cooper raises his glass. Everyone says his name in unison.

To Maverick.

Isaac smiles. George walks over to him and pulls out an envelope. "In this envelope are the keys and address to your new apartment." George's voice was deep. He stood 6 foot 5 and was very intimidating. "You don't pay rent. We pay your rent and all your bills. Electricity, water, garbage. There is a list in there where you go to buy food and which Doctor you go to if you're sick. Your Dentist and your Optometrist. All our people."

"I shop for food but don't pay for it?" Isaac whispers.

George nods. "We own the building. You just have to use check stand 1 always. All the instructions are in here on how to do things. No names. Just instructions. Read it. Memorize it. Burn it. You have three days. Understand?"

Isaac nods. "Do I live in a house or apartment?" Isaac asks. George looks at him. "I don't need to know."

"You're asking the same questions over and over," George told him. Isaac looks at the ground.

"Calm down," George tells him. "I was thinking where I should put you. You're asking good questions. I know this is overwhelming right now. Don't be scared anymore. You never have to be scared again. You have us now."

Isaac looks at him. He nods.

"You live in an apartment we got; somehow, I forgot from who or what." George waves his drink, which almost spills. Miriam chuckles.

"You have neighbors, Maverick," Miriam tells him. He turns his attention to her. "They will ask who you are and what you do. You tell them you're Maverick Henderson, and you're a Locksmith. You'll have the Van plus another car to drive on your days off. All the information you need to know will be in the envelope." Isaac nods.

Hunter walks over to Isaac. "Listen, if they ask you something you're not sure to answer, change the subject and sway the conversation away and let us know." Hunter pulls out a new cell phone. "This is your new phone. Never lose it. Keep it with you every day 24/7. Understand?" Isaac nods. "If you have any questions, text us. If you have any problems, text us if you need us. Text us."

"We'll always be here for you from this day forward," George says. "We're family now. And family sticks together."

George smiles and pats his shoulders. Isaac nods and smiles. He looks at Jerry, who gives him a thumbs-up.

Miriam gets up. "Dinner is almost ready, everyone. Let's gather in the dining room. Maverick, you come with me to the kitchen. I want to talk to you about one more thing," she instructs, and everyone leaves.

Isaac follows her and keeps repeating his name to familiarize himself. She watches him and smiles. In the large kitchen are two refrigerators. She opens one and then the other and looks disgusted. "Two refrigerators and no ice." She replies.

She holds up her drink. "I am a fool for ice in my drinks. Come with me to the ice box." Isaac follows her as she goes into the next room attached to the kitchen. The floor is concrete and there is meat hanging and an oak table to cut meat on. There is a wooden ice chest, and she opens it and uses the ice pick to pick some ice off.

Inside the ice chest lays two bodies and she makes sure that Isaac sees them. He does as his eyes widen. "We have our quarks, but we are a society. We do not care or judge each other whether we are fat or thin or young or old," Miriam begins. "We don't care if you're gay or straight or what your religion is. Looks mean nothing to us. We're all unique. We all bring something to the table when the opportunity arises, and it will. We have a Doctor who will take care of us if we're sick. We have a police captain to lose our paperwork when we get into trouble and a judge to back him up. We have a construction worker to hide the body and land to hide thousands more. We know how to dissolve a body or make a body appear in someone else's car if we need to. And if we don't have it here, we'll contact one of the other families in the other states to see if they have anyone we can use. After all, there are 50 states here to utilize."

Isaac digests that. He nods to Miriam. "I understand," he replies.

"One more thing, Maverick," she stands next to him and points at his chest. "Your parents still live here and are still alive. Under no circumstance are you to contact them and tell them who you are now."

"I understand. I won't." Isaac replies.

She nods. "Good," she points to the door out.

"What do I do on my days off?" Isaac asks. Miriam laughs.

"What do you like to do?" she asks him, humored by the questions.

"I don't want to ask something stupid, but I thought I would have to ask permission to do anything," Isaac asks.

She smiles. "No, dear. Most of us don't hang out other than for work or during our free time activities that we enjoy. So, if you like to bowl, then bowl. If you love movies, by all means, go to the movies. But always remember to keep the phone by you 24/7 in case anyone in the family needs you, whether it be seeing a prowler on their property or they get locked out."

Isaac nods and goes to the dining room with Miriam. Miriam points to a spot at the end of the table for Isaac, next to Jerry, who is trying to get his attention. The men all stand until Miriam sits then they all sit.

The meal is served, and Miriam raises her glass. "To family. Who cares if the world won't accept us for who we are. Why fit in when we are born to stand out."

Everyone cheers.

Chapter 13

Epilogue

Maverick looks out the window at the building he's being dropped off at. It was the new Condos in the wealthy part of town. He had driven by it several times the year before. "Wow," he says out loud.

"Nice, huh?" Cooper says, slapping his leg. "Inside the envelope is your room number, and you have two parking slots. One is for the Van, which is already parked there, and your other keys are on the table in the living room with the other information. You start work on Monday."

Maverick nods. "Do I pick up Jerry, or does he just show up here?" Maverick asks.

"Read the envelope," Cooper smiles. Maverick gets out of the car and waves at Cooper. Cooper rolls his window down. "You'll learn one thing about us. We are very thorough and think of everything."

Maverick waves and opens the envelope. On a card, it says 1100, and there is a set of keys. Nothing else is in the envelope. He walks into the lobby and is met with hellos. No one asks him if he belongs or what he is doing there. It's almost as if they all know.

He walks to the elevator and goes in. He looks at the numbers and realizes he's on the top floor. "No way," he says out loud and presses the top button. When the door opens, he looks at the door, which says 1100.

There is no other door on the floor. He opens the door and walks into his new condo. "I got the penthouse," he says out loud. He walks around, blown away by the elegant layout and stylish furniture. His fridge is stocked, and he even has a wine area.

He goes to the terrace and smiles. He goes right away to the table where the other envelope sits and reads everything on the paper.

Maverick Alexander Henderson, Age 18. Orphan. Foster Care. Parents John and Alice died in a car accident when Maverick was a baby. No other family. Locksmith by trade. Homeschooled. No siblings.

Maverick smiled. He was told it was an apartment, but he was living better than anyone his age. He looks at the list of where he's supposed to go and who he's supposed to see when he needs care. In the envelope are two sets of keys and another set of keys to match his Condo. Back-up set. Also in the envelope was a wallet full of cash, an ID with his new name and matching insurance card, gas card, and credit card. He counted five crisp $100 bills.

They told him he had a car also. He hears a noise in another room. A whimpering, he gets up and heads to the vacant room in the hall. He hadn't checked out all the extra rooms, so he quickly opened it to see what it was. The room is empty, and a box is on the floor. He looks at the open box and sees a small dog inside with a ribbon and a note attached. He picks the dog up, and the dog begins to lick his face over and over. He reads the note.

"Welcome home. We didn't want you to feel lonely. Meetings are at the end of each month. Attendance is mandatory. We named him Martin. Love Miriam."

Maverick smiles. He looks into each room. His bedroom was beautiful and masculine-looking. The other room was set up like a study. In the final extra room was a pool table and weights. He smiled. He looked at Martin and said, "Should we check out our car?"

Maverick took his elevator from his room to the garage attached. The van sat there, and next to the van was a covered car. Maverick smiled. He took the cover off and looked at the beautiful black Mustang. He nodded in improvement.

"Let's go for a ride, Martin," He said as he put his Corgi next to him. Martin settled in very nicely. Maverick slowly pulled out of the garage and took off. He rode to the corner, where he almost went through a red light. He chuckled to himself and looked to see if the car next to him saw.

Next to him in a blue station wagon were his parents. His mouth fell open. The woman looked at him in disgust and shook her head. His father made no eye contact. The light turned green, and they continued on. Shaken, Maverick drove to the ridge on the pathway where they first saw the Van and parked.

He looked up at the fire pit area and a group of new kids there starting a fire. He smiled. He looked around and nodded. No, he never got out of this town, but he was ok with that. He adjusted the mirror and looked at Martin.

"Well, Martin, we're here for life, but that's ok. Who cares if the world won't accept who we are, right? Why fit in when you were born to stand out." Maverick laughs. He peels out and toward whatever life and his new family would bring. Jerry smiles, sticks his hand out the sunroof, and flips off the world.

As they drive away a sign catches Mavericks eye. It shows a new development coming to the community. "200 more homes coming soon," the large billboard reads. Maverick laughs. He knew exactly who owned the land and who was moving in.

The
Black Notebook
Contents:
The 43

1. ROOSTER
2. LOL KILLER
3. Re-Run
4. Blade
5. Hacksaw
6. Grinder
7. Dr. Savage
8. Sandman
9. Jackal
10. Angel of Death
11. The Executioner
12. The Exterminator
13. Cupid
14. Wolf
15. Toy Maker
16. Widow Maker
17. Beans
18. Hands Malone
19. Auditor/Rat
20. Ice Pick
21. The Bear
22. The Counselor
23. The Mad Hatter
24. Thief of Hearts
25. Justice
26. Father Grime
27. Big John

28. Stone Killer
29. Dr. Slaughter
30. The Butcher (Slaughter House Killer) Tommy
31. Snowman
32. Packer
33. Light Keeper
34. Sledge
35. Timekeeper
36. Werewolf
37. Lonely Heart Killer
38. Lonely Heart Killer 2
39. Annihilator
40. Playing card killer
41. Watcher
42. The Preppie Killer
43. The Planner

ROOSTER

- Rooster is a black man who stands at 6 foot 2. Slender build. He hunts in the homeless camps, appearing as one of them.
- He recruits homeless children. Never to harm them but to protect them. He divides them into groups after intense testing.
- The smart ones he hides at night in the libraries so they can learn more and faster. He uses them as adults in the future. The tough ones he works with they become his soldiers. The weak ones are considered pawns. They do all the stealing and gathering for him.
- He hides the tough ones and weak ones in storage sheds in the city. This way they are still protected by the elements and the adults who would do them harm. They are taught how to survive and watch the streets for him.
- They bring him what they steal, and he pays for the storage sheds, clothes and food. In exchange for this, they receive protection, knowledge and education.
- Rooster loves M&M candies and is always eating them.
- He communicates by writing on the walls of alleys with yellow chalk.

- If anyone touches one of his kids, he will gut them with a large hunting knife that he carries under the leather trench coat he always wears.
- He has a mohawk that is colored red, like a rooster. To freak people out, he crows like a rooster, giving the impression that he is insane. He is not. When he was young, he worked in the armed forces, where he was educated in combat, survival skills and car mechanics.
- Rooster feels he is helping mankind by protecting the street children and getting them ready for adulthood.

LOL KILLER

- Little old lady Killer. She is an old lady in her early 80's. She looks fragile and wears clothes appropriate for her age. She slumps over when she's out in public giving the illusion she is feeble and weak. She is not.

- She changes her appearance from glasses and sometimes uses a cane or walker in her rouse to get homeless men to help her. Homeless men are her target of choice.

- She hates other women.

- She brings the men to her house, promising to take care of them. She often picks men who are sick or feeble. Men come with her freely. They see her as no threat or an easy target. Once inside her house, they are trapped.

- She gives them food and tea which is laced with a mild sedative. This makes them sleep, and she can control them easily. She then suggests a warm bath, and while they take a bath, she will wash their clothes. She often lays out a new seat shirt and pants for them to wear when they are done bathing.

- When they come out, she suggests a good night's sleep. As they sleep, a mist comes through a nebulizer on the table by the bed. It drugs them into a deep sleep where she can subdue them.

- She cuts off their limbs and feeds them to her pigs she has in a pen in the backyard. She puts their torso into a garbage sack and drops them off in apartment complex garbage bins around the city. She uses different ones so not to get caught. On the foreheads of her victims, she writes "LOL" with a black Sharpie.

RE-RUN

- ReRun is a male in his early 20's.

- He is very good-looking and narcissistic. He is constantly looking at himself in the mirror or any reflection he passes.

- He picks up women in bars, laundry mats, and stores. He is very charming, and women willing go out on a date with him. His preferred method of hunting is to get women from hotels. These women are from out of town and won't be missing immediately.

- He takes them on a date to a restaurant right off the outskirts of the city. Then he takes them to a secure area and beats them with the bunt end of his gun. He makes them undress from the waist down, humiliating them. He then continues to beat them until they lose consciousness.

- When they come to, they find themselves tied to a heavy piece of equipment or log so they cannot run away. He then runs them over with his car. He removes their ties and then runs them over again and again until they are dead.

- He places them in saran wrap and puts them into a remote part of the woods, where he rolls them over a cliff. Most of the bodies are found by animals who start to feed on them. Others by exposure to the weather. A few from hikers.

BLADE

- Blade is a Hispanic male in his late 20's. He is bald and covered in tattoos. He is heavy set and has large ear lobes with gages in them.

- Intimidating to see, but when he speaks, he has a soft voice and a lovely demeanor. He's very polite. He smiles a lot and is very helpful.

- He works in a nursing home as a nurse's aide. He sees the suffering of the elderly and the placement of them in nursing homes as a horrible choice made by families and society. He feels they should be at home surrounded by their families.

- He grew up in the foster care system and has no family in the USA. His family died while coving over the USA from Mexico illegally. His father died during the immigration, and his mother was raped in front of him as a child. Even though she suffered she continued and made the best life for him and his sister. She got sick and died from Cancer. She could not afford the meds, and Blade and his sister were taken away on put in separate homes.

- He lost contact with his sister, and his life was lonely, where he felt invisible, like the elderly people in the nursing homes he takes care of. He sees how visitors show up less and less as the years go by for them. When they do visit the time they spend with them is less and less.

- He kills the elderly people who he feels are suffering. He gives them Phenobarbital. As they nod off, he whispers to them, "Go to the light." He also reminds them that the true journey to God with great pain and suffering. He then kills them with a knife, stabbing them repeatedly until they die.
- "Now GOD will accept you into his kingdom, and you will suffer no more," is the last thing he tells each of them. He places a cross on their bodies and folds in their hands.
- He then places the bodies where the victim last visited before coming into the nursing home.

HACKSAW

- Hacksaw is a large, stout white male in his late 40's.
- He is a farmer. He grows corn and hay. In one section of his farm, he grows tall sunflowers.
- He wears overalls with a white T-shirt underneath in the winter months. In the summer months, he wears overall shorts and a white T-shirt.
- He is often smiling and has a sadistic giggle and laugh.
- He gets triggered by anyone who laughs or makes fun of him. He also gets upset if people cross his land either by walking through it or coming out of their cars to take pictures of themselves with his sunflowers.
- When he suspects intruders, he sends out his dogs to corner them in the fields. He then takes them to another part of his land, behind his house, away from the highway and places them in holes he has dug up for this purpose. He buries them up to their neck. He feeds and waters them until he has a row of victims. He then uses his tractor and runs them over while they are still alive.
- He always gives his victims a choice. Death by tractor or by a hacksaw.
- The city kids come several times a year to visit his farm to learn about farm life and pet the animals.

GRINDER

- Grinder is a 50-year-old Veteran who owns a tow truck company. He is a sadistic serial killer.

- He helps stranded people on the highway. He watches gas stations along the highway and rest stops for victims.

- He targets stray people. An unattended child is left in the car or wandering around while parents are in the rest stop or store. Even a person goes to the bathroom alone.

- He places Chloroform into a handkerchief and subdues them. He places them on a hidden floor in the back seat of his truck,

- He then places them in his workshop. Inside, he has a chair that is secured to the cement floor. He chains them to the chair and tortures them with a grinder.

- He starts with their fingers and then their hands. He then grinds their toes and their feet.

- He audio tapes all his tortures, often repeating their names. He keeps their money and destroys their credit cards.

- He will send the audio tapes to their families on the first-year anniversary of their deaths.

- He tows their cars to the next state and leaves them in remote areas, by a rest stop or a lake. He will dispose of the bodies in the opposite direction and leave them out in the woods for the animals to devour.

- He has a map in his office with push pins on where he left each car and person marked by a specific color. He uses a CB radio. He shows no emotion when he tortures.

DR. SAVAGE

- Dr. Savage is a 50-year-old psychiatrist. He is single and sees the world as a cesspool of troubled people. He finds fault in each person.

- He has OCD. His clothes and even his jeans are pressed. His house is immaculate. He is a minimalist. He has only two sets of dishes, glasses and utensils.

- He listens to his patients' problems weekly, and when he gets their trust, he tells them he's looking for help in some small way at his house or lake property. It is usually something that would take less than an hour, and then promises them they can fish on his property or use a boat and go onto the lake. He even entices someone with the promises of a free session with him.

- When they arrive at his home, he will spray them with a sedative, which causes them to lose consciousness. He then places them in one of the four rooms he uses as a torture chamber.

- He talks to them calmly, reminding them that this is all their fault. That all roads let them here to him. It was their choice.

- He will kill them by their fears. Heights, drowning, falling, spiders, etc… If they have no fears, then he will use basic torture to kill them.

- He plays classical music while killing them. His basement is soundproof. He keeps a videotape of each death so he can replay them and relive the experience.

SANDMAN

- The Sandman is a 30-year-old thin man. Gaunt looking. He is a chief.

- His father, also a serial killer, removed part of his tongue when he was younger. He was punished for interrupting his father's baseball game on TV. He then sewed his mouth shut.

- The Sandman wears a gastrostomy tube to get nutrition into him. His wounds on his mouth are healed, but when he goes into psychotic mode, he sews his own mouth shut.

- He often wears a scarf around his face to hide this. His coworkers know of his abuse and are very protective of him. His boss is a mobster and has huge respect for him. The Sandman is not part of the mob but is protected by them. They do not know of his secret life of murder.

- He goes after bullies. He will cut out their tongues and place them in the right hand so as to say, "Hold your tongue."

- He will also cut their eyes and place sand into their eye sockets. This means "you cannot see him."

- He is related to the Jackal, among other serial killers. He is also the Jackal's favorite sibling.

- He very rarely talks because of his sewn mouth but has been known to remove his own sutures and speak when he needs to. He will then sew his mouth shut again.

- He has liver disease and is slowly dying. His dream is to die by the ocean.

JACKAL

- The Jackal is in their 60's. The Jackal is a housekeeper serial killer. Hates pedophiles.
- Has a sadistic laugh. Dark sense of humor. Defiant. Abusive childhood. Related to the Sandman and other serial killers.
- The Jackal was separated from the other siblings and came from an orphanage in Germany. Raised by a serial killer and a pedophile.
- Lives and hunts in the PNW. Hid bodies in Washington State, Oregon, Idaho and Montana.
- Owns a kill van. A gift from a US Senator.
- Receives a list of pedophiles every month from a police officer in Washington. The Jackal will watch them for a few days and get close. Then, tazer them and place them in the kill van. They are given Ketamine. The Jackal then tattoos "Jackal" on their forehead with a tattoo gun. Then, both hands are removed and both eyes are removed.
- The hands being removed means they can no longer touch another child. The eyes removed means they can no longer see what's coming at them, and they are blind like they blindside the children they hunted themselves.
- The Jackal then releases them into the woods, where they wander off and eventually die alone.

Some will fall and die. Most get septic or die of shock. Each pedophile has a baggie stapled to their back outlining who they are and the crime they committed.

- Most of the families of the pedophiles never look after them because they are embarrassed at what their own children have done.

ANGEL OF DEATH

- AOD is a 50-year-old bald woman who is a nurse. She has worked all over the USA. She has worked in hospitals, nursing homes and in home care. She often moves when she is being investigated for her patients dying.
- She has several tattoos. She is very elegant and speaks softly but with lots of authority.
- She grew up on a farm and was given up to the state by her parents because they became afraid of her. She started killing animals on the farm at the age of 8.
- She started in the hospital, killing her patients by putting other patient's meds in the IV bags. When caught she would simply change her name and move to another location and begin again.
- She began to perfect her game. She would use another nurse's badge when they left it out and kill patients, making it look like they did it. Again, when getting close to being caught, she would simply change her name and move again.
- When she was being watched by management and had to play it safe, she would simply begin killing homeless people.
- When she kills the homeless, she takes the bodies to the "Executioner" who has an incinerator. The

Executioner is in love with her and has even branded her as his property. The Angel of Death is in love with "The Counselor" and has a secret child with him.

- The Executioner is the Angel of Death's father.
- The Counselor is her brother.

THE EXECUTIONER

- The Executioner is in his 70's. He is 6 foot 8.
- He is very intimidating and sadistic. He is a child psychologist.
- He has 32 children. He has killed 26 of his children in many sadistic ways. All his children came from prostitutes.
- The Counselor and the Angel of Death are his favorite children.
- He oversees the community of Serial Killers. His brother is also a serial killer named "The Exterminator."
- He hates prostitutes. He will sleep with them, trying to impregnate them. If they don't give him the baby, he will kill them sadistically. If they do give him the children, he will let them live until the child bonds with him. He will then decide if they are worthy enough to be in the Agency with him. If they do not meet his expectations, he will kill them brutally.
- He runs "The Agency." A network of 2000 serial killers who plan to take over the judicial system in the United States of America. With crime in America at its worst and the judicial system falling apart, the Executioner plans to use criminals to take control of the crime and punishment in America. By having everyday Americans rely on him instead of

the court systems with its corrupt judges and lawyers or the government, it gives criminals a free ride to commit the murders that they love to do, and crime goes down 90%.

- Uses old methods to kill. A guillotine and body stretcher, among other items.
- His living children, in order are:
- The Jackal, The Counselor, Mad the Hatter, Angel of Death, Re-Run and Sandman.
- He is responsible for drowning the Jackal at age 2. He burned ½ of the Hatter's body. He branded the Angel of Death and rapes her. He is responsible for removing Sandman's tongue.
- He is hated and feared by everyone in his family.

THE EXTERMINATOR

- The Exterminator is a large man in his 70's. He is married, but his wife does not participate in the Agency's deeds. She knows about it but stays with him out of loyalty. They have two children who are also part of the Agency. Hacksaw and Cupid.
- The exterminator is his brother.
- He kills people who break the law and get away with it. He feels they will never change and do nothing for society.
- He has an electric chair in his basement in a special room he created. Along the walls are other torture devices.
- Hacksaw is his favorite child. He pays no attention to Cupid.
- He wants to gain control of the Agency but is intimidated by his older brother. He wants Hacksaw to run everything.
- He is not as powerful or intimidating as his brother, so no one sees him as a threat.

CUPID

- Female in her late 40's.
- Has daddy issues. Hates men.
- Loves and protects her brother but is jealous of the attention he gets.
- Never married.
- Uses a crossbow to kill men. She is very beautiful and seductive but very psychotic. Has a sadistic laugh. Has lots of tattoos and wears gothic clothing.
- She bates men into the woods to make out and then gives them a drink laced with a muscle relaxer. She ties them to a tree and shoots them with her bow and arrow while laughing sadistically as they die. She will often videotape the entire ordeal and replay it to relive it.
- When they are dead, she carves out their hears and, shoves it into their mouths and takes a picture. She has her own dark room and leaves pictures around town for people to see.

WOLF

- Large man in his 50's. Loner. Wears jeans and flannels. Smokes heavily and drinks alcohol.

- Mother was a prostitute who hated men and took it out on him. Makes him stand at the dinner table naked in front of his siblings, watching them eat. She beats him and dehumanizes him at every chance.

- He is adopted by a police officer who arrives at the house with CPS after school, and a neighbor report the mom. The Wolf learns the inner workings of the police station and has access to information that he provides to the Agency.

- He abuses women. He rapes them with objects and then dehumanizes them by shaving their heads and eyebrows off.

- He castrates himself so he can never have children.

- He considers any abuse of an animal to be death. He is always surrounded by either Shepherds, Dobermans or Pitbulls.

- He targets fishermen and hunters using the same items they use to hunt/fish to kill them. He then throws them into the river or leaves them in the woods for the animals to feed off of.

TOY MAKER

- A thin, tall man in his 70's. Always wears a suit. Carries a briefcase with him everywhere.

- Looks poor and gaunt but is very rich.

- Makes handmade toys and gives them to homeless children.

- He is very sadistic and smiles all the time.

- He displays his toys, and when kids see them, they come to him. He waits for the parents to come after the children, tells the parents he sees their kids and points toward the woods where his van is. Or down an alley by his van. He then kidnaps the parents. Most of his victims are street kids. He tells the parents he can offer them a better life.

- He breaks the parents' limbs. He uses Anectine, a paralytic, to subdue them. He then amputates their limbs, reattaches them backwards, places them into shopping carts, and leaves them in mall parking lots at night. (Arms to legs and vice versa)

- He is creating his own family that he never had. He sends the kids to school and gives them the love they never had. The kids gave him the family he never had.

WIDOWMAKER

- Plain looking male in his 40's.
- Abandoned by his own parents. Placed in Foster care and abandoned four more times by various families.
- He tries to be perfect.
- Killed a sibling for attention.
- He trolls the malls looking for vulnerable children. He chooses one who is left to roam the malls by themselves or who is easily manipulated to follow him out the door.
- He will sometimes find a child and follow them home and watch their family. He spends a lot of time surveying and manipulates himself into the family by a rouse. Often renting a house nearby, walking a dog, saying he's in the neighborhood (a block away) or joining the same club the wife/mother attends. Even shopping in the same store so, they end up running into each other.
- Once in the family's home, he kills the husband and takes over the family, becoming the father of that child. He moves from family to family after the woman grows tired of him or the child figures him out. He ends up killing the entire family, never finding his own.

BEANS

- Male in his 40's.
- He is the accountant for the Agency. He invests and gambles money.
- His gambling addiction causes him to lose a large quantity of money for the agency.
- He is found out and placed into a large glass container in the middle of the room. He is placed naked inside and let too slowly die in front of all to see as an example of what will happen if you turn on the Agency.
- Before he was caught, he tried to set up a fellow gambler as the fall guy. However, since the other gambler was out of town in Vegas during his spree he is caught. The Agency fears anyone catching onto them, so they make an example out of him.
- His house is given to the next accountant, who is put up for the job. There is a picture of Beans in that house of him naked inside the glass jar so the new accountant knows not to cross the Agency.

HANDS MALONE

- A large, intimidating man in his 30's.
- One of the handlers in the Agency. Abusive. Sadistic. Killed both his parents when he was in his teens.
- Discovered by the Executioner when given a psych eval in the juvenile system. The Executioner evaluation let him be in Juvie instead of adult court, saving him years in the system. In exchange, Hands Malone became the arm of the Agency under the Executioner.
- He is loyal to the Agency. He takes pleasure in beating people to death. He is patient and talks very calmly to his victims.
- Uses zip ties around the neck when he tosses bodies into the river. It becomes his signature.
- In his free time, he goes back into his past, killing those he feels has wronged him. Kids from school who made fun of him. Teachers, neighbors and even relatives said he would be nothing or never helped him.

AUDITOR/RAT

- Man in his 40's. Looks like a weasel.
- Values integrity. Very strict to his wife and two kids. He abuses them. When he makes a mistake, he has them abuse him.
- He is the one who turned in Beans.
- He kills those who break the rules. He kidnaps them and has his family watch as he kills them. He kills in his basement. His children and wife begin to join in, and it brings them all closer together as a family.
- He is very loyal to the Agency. Does all the accounting for the Agency.
- Idolizes the Executioner and the Exterminator.

ICE PICK

- Large burly man in his 40's.
- Hates everyone on the planet. Shows no emotion,
- Muscle for the Agency.
- Uses ice picks to the brain or to the ears of his victims.
- If he sees anyone laughing or having a good time and they happen to look in his direction, he thinks they are making fun of him, and he targets them.
- He will drive his car at night without lights on, and if an oncoming car flashes him with their lights, he will make him his next target.
- He leaves the victim without pants or underwear in the same place he kills them, showing them he thinks nothing of them and dehumanizes them.

THE BEAR

- Males in his 30's. Large, burly man.
- Garbage man.
- Part owner of a junkyard. The Agency uses its junkyard to get rid of bodies and demolish cars they've used in crimes.
- Targets and kills self-entitled people. Takes them to his junkyard and kills them by torture in different ways. He will carve them up and put them in ice chests. Then, sell body parts online on the dark web or in a hidden chat room.
- Puts body parts that are left over either in the garbage can around the city or in the junkyard compressor. He will even put them in abandoned cars about to be demolished.

THE COUNSELOR

- Tall, thin, well-dressed man in his 50's. Always wears an Armani suit.
- He is the Lawyer for the Agency. Charismatic but sadistic. Intense and direct.
- Unmarried but is sleeping with his sister, The Angel of Death. They have a secret child.
- Tasers his victims. He shoots his victims to wound but not kill. He then takes them into the woods, where he has placed barrels. He places them inside and then hammers the lid on top of them. He will drill a hole and pour acid on them. He laughs while they scream.

THE MAD HATTER

- Male in his 50's.
- Stands 6 foot 5. Tall and thin. Wears a top hat every time he goes out. Very elegant. Has an evil smile.
- He has burns on ½ side of his face. He wears a mask to cover.
- Listens to classical music.
- He is a lawyer.
- Was adopted by a billionaire before returning to his father and joining the Agency.
- Kills parents who abuse their children. Uses a double-sided sword that is four feet long. One side has a knife, which he uses to stab his victim, and the other side is a Katana, which he uses to decapitate his victim.
- He hangs out with the Jackal and the Angel of Death.

THIEF OF HEARTS

- Female in her 20's.
- She is a lonely, beautiful and romantic woman.
- She likes to join new churches and clubs and invites church people, salespeople who knock on her door and even the homeless to her home. She entertains them and then spikes their tea.
- They watch as she places a tarp on the floor of the kitchen and then places a chair on top of the tarp. She will then guide the drugged victim to the chair, where she uses zip ties to restrain them.
- She tells them romantic stories she fantasies about herself as she does this. She then cuts their ankles as they bleed out, telling them, "But you couldn't love and accept me the way I am."

JUSTICE

- A male in his 30's is a police officer.
- Very loyal to the Agency. Believes what the Agency is doing is bettering mankind. Keeps them updated on what is happening within the city and also when Detectives are onto them.
- Very sadistic.
- Offers rides to hitchhikers and then takes them to the lake or the woods and kills them. Knows where the location of cameras are located in these areas, so he's always under the radar.
- He uses a taser. Then beats, stabs and dehumanizes them before killing them. He plants drugs on them that he steals from dealers and other convicts to make it look like they are on drugs or dealing drugs when their bodies are found.
- He's in love with Cupid.

FATHER GRIME

- Males in his 50's.
- Priest.
- He targets homeless camps.
- He goes to the outskirts of town to find straggler homeless groups and targets them. He comes in non-threatening by dressing as a priest and offering services and prayers to them.
- He will lock them up in their own tents. He then pours light fluid over the tent and lights it on fire while reading scripture.
- If the homeless person is just in a sleeping bag, he will spray the bag full of lighter fluid and then light them up and sing while they burn to death.

BIG JOHN

- Male in his early 60's.
- Trucker
- Average build. Wears Jeans and T-shirts or flannel shirts.
- Picks up both male and female hitchhikers.
- He will use a Taser or ketamine. He then takes them into the woods and ties them to a tree. He will shoot them with a BB gun for fun. When he's done with his game of torture, he'll pull out a pistol crossbow. After killing his victims, he removes the crossbows and cleans them to use on the next victim.
- He keeps his victims tied to the tree. He has a unique way of tying his rope which becomes his signature.

STONE KILLER

- Males in his early 20's.

- Average looking.

- Befriends and picks up homeless men and women, and prostitutes.

- He takes them out to eat or for a drive just to talk and then returns them. As they walk away, he hits them with a rock.

- He is considered a coward by the other serial killers because he kills his victims while their backs are turned. You must always face those you are about to kill.

- He has a price on his head from other serial killers. They are bidding on which one gets to kill him for sport.

DR. SLAUGHTER

- Males in his late 40's who is a doctor.
- He offers low-cost surgery for homeless and poor people under-the-table procedures for cash only.
- He operates on people while they are awake. He removes their body parts and sells them to rich people. (Kidney, liver, eyes)
- He has a kill van that he operates in. He drives down the street in it and has music come from it like an ice cream truck.

THE BUTCHER (SLAUGHTERHOUSE KILLER) TOMMY

- Male teen.
- 6 foot 3. Farm kid.
- Began killing after watching his father, grandfather, and uncles hunt, skin and drain the blood of deer. He watched as they hung them and gutted them. He began to play in the blood.
- This triggered something inside him, and he began to kill some of the farm animals until his uncle and grandfather started to get concerned. He switched to rodents and small animals like rabbits and squirrels.
- His grandfather started following him and saw him kill an animal, and the joy it brought him brought it to the attention of the family. The doctor gave him a psych eval, and the conclusion was that Tommy would become a serial killer one day.
- Grandma and Mom refused to buy into this, but the men agreed with the doctor and signed the papers for Tommy to be committed and get help. When he turned 18, he was released from the Psych hospital and came home and killed his entire family.
- The Executioner kept tabs on Tommy since he was the one who evaluated him for the courts. The Executioner invites Tommy to join the Agency.

Tommy refuses, saying he only wants to kill randomly and as often as he wants.

- He almost gets caught, but the Agency saves him. Finally, Tommy does join when he realizes that the Agency will always kill and he will always have a family to rely on. He gives them his loyalty.

SNOWMAN

- Males in his 30's.
- Has white hair and is heavy-set.
- Has an ice cream truck and trolls the parks schools. He looks for runaways and homeless shelters for children.
- When he sees kids he gets out of the truck to play hide and seek with them. He dresses colourfully and smiles a lot. He is childlike, and kids go to him. He gives them laced candy and kills the children. He leaves them in dumpsters around the town.
- The Agency does not like the Snowman and wants him to leave the community. He draws the attention of the authorities.

PACKER

- Male in his 40's.
- Woodsman.
- Breaks into campers and steals their food, money and anything of value. They are usually fishing or hiking when he does this. He cuts their tyres and breaks their gas and brake lines. This causes them to be stranded or break down.
- He then emerges as a helper. He ties them up, puts them into a barrel, and nails it shut. He drills a hole and pours spiders and bugs. He listens to his victims scream in horror. He then pours lighter fluid on top of the barrel, lights it on fire and lets it burn to death.
- He videotapes the whole ordeal to watch later and relive the experience over and over.

LIGHTKEEPER

- Males in his 60's.
- Average height and build.
- Looks like a retired, tan golfer.
- Pretends to have Dementia. Gets people to help him, and then he tasers them three times in their car. Gives Ketamine to them and drives them out of town to a lake and drowns them.
- If the victim is a male, he drowns them immediately.
- If the victim is a female, he will resuscitate and repeat until their hearts go out.

SLEDGE

- Male in his mid-50s.
- Very thin and gaunt. Dresses dark. Fits in with the homeless.
- He's actually very rich.
- He hangs with the homeless and gains their trust. Goes after the stragglers who leave the group to go out on their own. Kills them with a hammer.
- The homeless eventually figured out it was him and gave him an OD of meth. He survives the attempt and winds up in a nursing home. The homeless go to the Angel of Death and ask for her help.
- Even though Sledge is a member of the Agency, the homeless promise to help the Agency with news and chatter on the streets; this outweighs anything Sledge has done. They also promise to help with the police and the FBI.
- Sledge is killed by the Angel of Death, and his death is videotaped and given to the Homeless as a promise of their bond with the Agency.

TIMEKEEPER

- Male in his 40's.
- Businessman by day and a bar hopper by night.
- He befriends drunk males and females at bars. Walks them to their cars and invites them back to his house to sleep it off or have another drink.
- Once inside his house, it's like a puzzle and they can't get back out of the house.
- He gives his victims only 2 hours to figure out how to get out of the house before he electrocutes them. No one ever makes it out alive.

WEREWOLF

- Males in his 50's.
- Large, burly man who hitch-hikes.
- When picked up, he has a soft, inviting voice and kind eyes. His hair is kept, so he appears safe.
- He will taser the driver immediately and take him to a remote area. He then shoots his victim in the leg or arm. He has the victim's ID cards/wallet/keys. He then releases his victims and tells them to run, and he hunts them down like an animal and kills them.

LONELY HEART KILLER

- Woman in her 30's.
- Plain looking.
- Goes to church meetings and social events for single lonely people to hook up with others.
- She will invite the man over immediately, promising a good time. Gives them sleepy Tea and takes all their ID/cash/jewellery.
- She puts them in a wheelbarrow and into the remote woods. She buries them alive in the woods with the help of her mute husband.
- She then takes their cars and abandons them in a mall parking lot or at the airport.

LONELY HEART KILLER 2

- Twin of the first woman. Has the same first name.
- Goes only to bereavement meetings.
- With the help of her twin, she buries the bodies along with her husband.
- She will convince people who are grieving to commit suicide. Has them write their own obituaries. If they don't, she says she understands and offers them some sleepy Tea. Then, put the gun in their hands and, using their hands, guide them to commit suicide while they watch themselves in the mirror's reflection.

ANNIHILATOR

- Male in his 50's.
- Homeless drifter.
- Wanders through the woods where campsites are. He makes kids kill their parents and then kills the kids after living out the fantasy of them being siblings.

PLAYING CARD KILLER

- Male in his mid-30s.
- Churchman who befriends the homeless and runaways.
- He brings them home and feeds them. Let them use his shower.
- They only must play cards with him. He plays with a regular card deck, but after one hand, he trades the cards for a special deck.
- Each card is a type of torture, and he does that to the person depending on which care he turns over or which card they pick.

WATCHER

- Male in his 40's.
- 2nd generation serial killer.
- He roams the highways looking for those who are stranded.
- Will stop at scenic sites to pretend to look at them. He will walk over to cars in the lots and pop holes in the tyres, causing them to be stranded. He has a knife inside his right boot he uses.
- Then, he will slowly follow them till they pull over on the side of the road. He tows them to the shop he owns to fix the tyre for free. He kidnaps the driver and passenger and even sometimes whole families. He places them in his shed on the back of the property and tortures them for hours and sometimes for days.
- He records the torture and then sends the tapes to their families so they can share the experience with him.

THE PREPPIE KILLER

- Males in his early 30's.
- Became a forever college student. Takes every class available. Never graduates. He has no friends because everyone eventually moves on with their lives except him. His family pays for him to stay away.
- He finds old yearbooks in Thrift shops and looks up the popular kids and finds them and kills them. They have the lives he wishes he had.
- He leaves them nude and in a compromising position to embarrass and humiliate them. (dog collars)

THE PLANNER

- Male in his late 80's.
- Tall and gaunt. Looks like a mortician.
- Pretends to work for the cemetery and follows up with customers who have recently lost family members. He follows them from the cemetery where he is a groundskeeper and sometimes from the paper if they went to a different cemetery.
- He also works in the hospital as an orderly.
- He takes a notebook with him everywhere and writes down information on the families of those who let him in the house.
- Once inside, he goes to the bathroom and opens a window to sneak in later in the evening. He smothers the grieving family member with a pillow and steals their items.
- He is finally caught by a teenager who annihilates him.
- The Agency invites him to join and covers up what he does.

Outro

I grew up in this community. It's where our family ended up at. Where I would fit in. I would be with others who were just like me.

It was also a place where I could learn and grow and evolve. Where you grew up and went to church, played on playgrounds, went to the mall, to movies and on family vacations.

I went to neighbor's houses and learned how to steal, drive a car, outrun the police, pick a lock, and stab someone slowly so their death would take longer be more painful. I learned how to remove a lung or a heart out of the body and to take someone's life without any hesitation.

I could dissolve a body and hide a body anywhere. My education was different than yours. While you might have these thoughts once or twice in your life. I lived these thoughts freely out in the open.

Free to be myself. I also went to the mall and to the movies. When you did, you went to enjoy the movie. I went to hunt. I lived the movie.

You painted with crayons and watercolors. I painted with blood.

I did a self-portrait of myself. I'll post it below. This is my self-portrait of me….the Jackal at age 7. Right after my first kill. I'll now tell you about my teen years. Those are more interesting. Are you ready?

Address to the Jackal:

Jackal

6325 N Monroe Street

Po box 48111

Spokane, Wa.

99208-9998

www.ingramcontent.com/pod-product-compliance
Lightning Source LLC
Chambersburg PA
CBHW071926150726
47999CB00001B/116